Letters from Hindustan

Letters from Hindustan

Stories of Hope from Around the Country

Kopal Khanna

JUGGERNAUT BOOKS
C-I-128, First Floor, Sangam Vihar,
Near Holi Chowk, New Delhi 110080, India

First published by Juggernaut Books 2025

Copyright © Kopal Khanna 2025

10 9 8 7 6 5 4 3 2 1

P-ISBN: 9789353454708
E-ISBN: 9789353455477

All rights reserved. No part of this publication may be reproduced, transmitted, or stored in a retrieval system in any form or by any means without the written permission of the publisher.

Typeset in Adobe Caslon Pro by
R. Ajith Kumar, Noida

Printed at Thomson Press India Ltd

To Majnu, my late beloved dog,
who taught me love and empathy

Contents

Introduction — 1

Story 1 — 11
I Launched a Start-Up at 87 During the Pandemic
USHA GUPTA

Story 2 — 21
The *Suhaag Raat* That Wasn't
PALLAVI JAIN

Story 3 — 35
The Stranger Who Proved Me Wrong About Trust
PRIYA MALIK

Story 4 — 47
I Am a Trans Woman and I Found My Soulmate
DANIELLA MENDONCA

Story 5 — 59
Why Do All These Slum Girls Dress Like Boys?
SALONI KAPOOR

CONTENTS

Story 6   69
How I Overcame Tragedy and Won
Gold for India
EKTA BHYAN

Story 7   79
The Last Gift My Brother Left Me
SHWETA SHARMA

Story 8   91
If Karma Exists ... Is It Always a 'Bitch'?
RASHMI KURUP

Story 9   101
How I Fought Back After My Husband
Threw Acid on Me
MEENA SONI

Story 10   111
How Blindness Led Me to Conquer
Mountains
MANDAVI GARG

Story 11   123
The Day My Great-Grandmother Chose
to Die – Then Lived
MAHITHA

Story 12
How One Promise Took Me to the
Families of 1,000 Soldiers
VIKAS MANHAS
137

Story 13
He Texted Me His Last Words – But I'll
Never Get a Reply
SYLVINA JENNIFER
149

Story 14
I Have a Prosthetic Leg – But I Decided
to Become a Dancer
SUSHMITA CHAKRABORTY
157

Story 15
The Eid Journey That Reconnected Me
With Humanity
NAUSHEEN KHAN
169

Story 16
Why the 'Perfect Wedding' Isn't as Perfect
as We Think
SHRUTI SONAL
177

Story 17
I Wanted to Be Tendulkar, But That
One Day Changed My Life
KRISHNA IYER
191

CONTENTS

Story 18   205
How Speaking Up Saved Me
AARTI KUBER

Story 19   217
How a Simple Auto Ride Changed
My Life Forever
RITIKA SONI

Story 20   229
Does Anyone Have an Extra Pen?
A Story of Friendship and Loss
DUSHYANT SINGH

Story 21   241
The Day I Pretended To Be an Alcoholic
EISHA CHOPRA

Story 22   257
I Am a Police Officer, But This Is
My True Legacy
THAN SINGH

Your Takeaways   271
Acknowledgements   273
A Note on the Author   277

Introduction

Story.

Well, allow me to start with one. Actually, three.

It was 2013, and I was volunteering with an organization in my home town, Lucknow. My internship entailed documenting the impactful work done by the organization. Everything was going well until my supervisor informed me of a change in plans. She needed someone's help with the Jail Programme – a unit within the organization that focuses on improving the lives of women inmates by upskilling them and enabling them to rebuild their lives once they are out of jail. The English teacher who worked with the inmates was ill and would not be able to take her regular sessions for some time. So, my supervisor asked me if I'd be okay to fill in. Of course I said yes. I was barely 20 and open to new experiences, even though a part of me was scared. I'd seen jails in movies and read about criminals in newspapers, but I'd never really met one in real life. Naturally, I had several apprehensions, not the least being the thought of teaching them English. It was daunting in more ways than one.

The jail was an hour-long drive away. My mentor, Meena Ma'am, asked me, 'How are you feeling?' I told her the truth, but she didn't say anything to me then. No words of consolation. No 'You will be okay'.

We reached the jail, completed all the formalities, surrendered our phones and walked in. It was nothing like I had ever imagined. It was open, spacious and clean. We walked into a room that had been labelled 'The Pathshala' but it was empty. Just then a bell rang from somewhere deep inside the compound and

INTRODUCTION

about 30 women, giggling and clearly full of excitement, walked in. Some of them, I noticed, were holding a child.

Settling down quickly, several of them asked in unison, 'Ma'am, *aaj kya padhenge*? (What will we study today?)' Meena Ma'am introduced me, and they welcomed me. It was not a regular, impersonal welcome. It was a heartfelt one, full of warmth and sisterhood – like how you would welcome your favourite person into your house, thrilled that they were there. I was quiet for most of the session until a middle-aged woman walked up to me and said, '*Aap mujhe angrezi padhaoge*?' (Will you teach me English?) I was nervous but I smiled and said, 'Haan,' and the woman beamed with happiness. She added, '*Yaha se bahar nikal jau, phir job karungi.*' (Once I'm out of here, I will take up a job.)

On our way back to the office, Meena Ma'am smiled and asked me, 'How are you feeling now?' I remember telling her something about stories, about how important it is for people to tell their own stories. This was day one of four months of getting to meet the women from whom I'd draw strength even ten years later.

In 2016, I began working on Tape A Tale. The idea was to create an audio platform where people could record their personal stories in their voices and share them with the world. I knew this was what I wanted to do, but I didn't know who would tell stories on this platform or where I would find these people. I spent the initial days finding my first few storytellers from within my small network of friends and family. That is when my friend told me about her cousin, who had just ended her marriage with an abusive man. She thought it would be a good idea for me to talk to her and gave me her number. I got on a call with her, told her about my plans to start a storytelling platform and asked if she'd be comfortable sharing her story on my platform.

'I'm not a good storyteller, but I would like to tell my story,' she told me. I asked her to take her time and send me the story whenever she

INTRODUCTION

was ready. Later that night, I received a seven-minute-long voice note from her on WhatsApp. It was her story – raw, honest and impactful. She spoke about her arranged marriage, how her in-laws tortured her for dowry and how her husband abused her. She had finally gathered the courage to file for divorce. Her story was hard-hitting. Before I could thank her for sharing it with me, I received another message from her saying, 'Thank you.' I felt overwhelmed. She said she had been trying to find some kind of closure for over two years, and the process of narrating her story to me, just saying it all out loud, had made her see her journey in a way she hadn't seen before. She wanted to share the story so that women like her could find the courage to let go. The courage she showed that day made me wonder if stories really have that kind of power – to shake things up, to drive people to action.

As time passed, we wove together one story after another, and slowly but steadily built a community of over three million people. We started doing events where people could come and share their stories – soon the videos of storytellers narrating their stories started reaching millions of people.

In 2022, I got a call from one of our most loved storytellers, Rakesh Tiwari. He had been sharing his stories on our platform for over three years. But that day he didn't call to tell me his story, but that of Rahul, one of his fans. Rahul had lost his mother when he was 20 and blamed his father for it, to the extent that they hadn't spoken properly with each other for over eight years despite living under the same roof. One fine afternoon, while the father and son were watching the IPL highlights on a computer, Rakesh Tiwari's video on Tape A Tale appeared on their screen as a suggestion and began to play on YouTube. The story, 'Yaadon Ka Swaad', was about how he lost his father and how all that remained was the bittersweet taste of his memories in the form of samosas that his father

INTRODUCTION

loved to eat and feed. Once the five-minute story was over, a teary-eyed father got up from the sofa and went to his room quietly. Sensing his tears, the son followed him, and just like that, what hadn't happened in eight years, transpired – they hugged each other and cried. I could sense Rakesh's emotions as he told me this. I could hear his voice crack. His throat clenched. Before ending the call, he said, 'Stories are so powerful, Kopal. They hold the ability to heal both the teller and the listener.'

With this hope in my heart, I present to you *Letters from Hindustan*, a collection of stories from India, by the people and for them. As you leaf through these pages, I hope you discover yourself in the words of individuals you may never meet, but who may not seem like strangers at all. I hope this book embraces you like a warm hug on a cold winter evening. I hope it grants you the courage to find love, heal a broken heart, overcome adversity, look into someone's eyes and express your true feelings, climb that mountain despite fearing its vastness and solitude, brighten someone's day and, most importantly, create space for people to share their honest stories.

Whether their version resonates with you or not, whether the people resemble you or not, whether they speak like you or not, let's make room for stories to breathe because, in the end, it is only stories that will endure. And as long as people can tell their stories without fear, hope will continue to thrive.

Story 1

I Launched a Start-Up at 87 During the Pandemic

USHA GUPTA

My husband, Rajkumar ji, and I had been married for 63 years in 2021. I was 24 when I married him. I was still learning how the world worked, so having him by my side felt like having a constant companion to guide and support me through life. I sought his opinion on everything, even when it wasn't his area of expertise, because I trusted him completely. He cared for me so deeply that life seemed to revolve around us being together. Rajkumar ji and I really did grow old together. We got married, had children, watched our kids become parents themselves, and our favourite part of this journey was becoming Nana and Nani. Sixty-three years isn't a short time. When I see young couples today taking vows to grow old together, it fills my heart with joy.

In 2021, during the second wave of the pandemic, the world changed. We were visiting our daughter in New Delhi when both Rajkumar ji and I tested positive for COVID-19 and were admitted to the hospital. We were placed in the same ward, but while I was doing slightly better, Rajkumar ji was in immense discomfort and pain. It broke my heart to see him suffer, and I prayed every day for his recovery. For three weeks, the suffering around us was overwhelming. People were losing their loved ones, were unable to meet their parents and children, and critically ill patients were struggling to find beds in the hospitals. The pain and despair were palpable. There were so many younger people who desperately needed those hospital beds. I couldn't help but think about our ages – I was 87 and Rajkumar ji was over 90.

I wished that my husband would miraculously feel better, but life, as it always does, had other plans. After battling the gruesome disease for three weeks, he passed away. Six decades of living with someone – what would life be without him by my side? I had no idea. I didn't even want to know.

Life came to a standstill. I had been so dependent on my husband for everything, and now, everything reminded me of him. I couldn't shake the memories of what I had witnessed during those weeks in the hospital – the overwhelming pain and despair that filled within those walls. I couldn't save my husband, but I kept wondering – what could I do to help someone else who was suffering?

Make achaar (pickle).

That was my answer or rather my granddaughter's answer when I told her I wanted to do something to help people suffering in the pandemic. My husband had loved the pickles I made at home. Not just my husband; my grandchildren looked forward to Nani's pickle jars every year. I wanted to donate some money but my grandchildren suggested I do what I do best; they said make achaar, sell it and help people in need with the proceeds. I knew they suggested this to keep me busy, but as timing would have it, the mango season was in progress and I didn't have any reason to say no.

So in the memory of my husband and for the people suffering, I decided to help by making Nani's delicious home-made pickles and chutneys. That's how 'Pickled with Love' was born; my first start-up at the age of 87. The first time in my life I was doing something of my own. My team? My children and my grandchildren. From naming the organization and designing the cutest logo to sourcing jars and making an Instagram page to market the products, they stood by me throughout this journey. I worked tirelessly and made sure to achieve my targets for each day.

I knew every jar of pickle mattered because every penny collected through its sale mattered. A 200 gram bottle of pickle or chutney costs ₹150. Every penny we collected from every bottle we sold, my grandchildren, Radhika and Abhinav, helped me donate the money through an NGO called Every Infant Matters. The proceeds would go to families who needed money for rations, medicine bills or to just survive through the pandemic.

In a few months, my business helped more than 65,000 homeless people across four cities to get their meals. All the money earned went towards COVID-19 relief and other such charitable projects that help mobilize resources for those in need. I felt like I had found a purpose in life when I had lost all hope. The messages from these families would light up my eyes.

My husband always told me, 'Whatever you do, Usha, do it with all your heart,' and that's exactly what I tried to abide by. Today the pandemic is behind us but my memories of our time at the hospital aren't. I want to keep helping people.

Building something of my own at 87 felt so surreal. It made me fall in love with myself and my capabilities. Today, I want to empower underprivileged women and train them to start small businesses of their own. I want to help them learn the art of cooking to earn a livelihood.

From just being Usha Gupta and Nani to my grandchildren to becoming Nani to thousands out there, this journey has been incredibly beautiful. What started with 'Nani, you cook so well' has now grown to serve thousands.

People around me tell me that I should rest; spend the rest of my life in peace, but they don't know that this is peace for me now. Age, honestly, is just a number. I'm still writing new chapters in my life, opening new doors of opportunity and living each day with zest and wonder. I've achieved things in the twilight of my life that I could never have dreamt of as a young girl, and for this experience, I will remain forever grateful.

My heart misses Rajkumar ji every day but I am very certain today that wherever he is, he is happy to see me, surrounded and pickled with love.

Kopal's Takeaway

Usha ji is a true hero. Not the kind that smashes glasses in our movies or performs grand gestures, but the kind that quietly transforms the most challenging circumstances into something beautiful. She's a testament to resilience, creativity and love. Her story will always remind us that when life takes an unexpected turn, we are still the ones driving the car. Even in the face of loss and hardship, Usha ji showed us that it's never too late to find a new purpose, to give and to keep moving forward with grace and determination. Her journey is a shining example of how strength can bloom from the most unlikely places.

Story 2

The *Suhaag Raat* That Wasn't

PALLAVI JAIN

This is not the story of my *suhaag raat* (my wedding night or golden night) but the story of someone from whom all her light had been stolen; of someone whose radiance had been diminished and whose freedom over her own body had been restrained; a story I had not sought but one that found me.

'Didi, please tell me, what do couples do on their first night?' I reluctantly asked a community health worker in the semi-urban area of Madanpur Khadar in Delhi; I had set out on a research mission to collect stories about family planning from across the country. I didn't want to sound like I was prying into her intimate life so I decided to use my upcoming marriage as a cue to break the ice with Didi. She was in her mid-forties. Sitting on the floor, bored and hot on a scorching June afternoon as the ceiling fan seemed to take its very last breath, my query made Didi's eyes light up. She now wore a bright smile. 'You are twenty-six years old and about to be married and you still don't know what to do on your golden night?' Seeing the puzzled look on my face she instantly said, 'Arre, golden night, meaning your honeymoon night. The night when you will be legally allowed to break all sexual shackles and feel free to live life.' Giggling meekly over Didi's animated gestures, I felt too shy to let her in on my own life.

As we talked, our conversation was interrupted by the tinkling of Aarti's glass bangles and silver anklets. Aarti, 28, was short and subdued in her demeanour, but as soon as she walked in, she whipped away the sari pallu covering her face, revealing her bright, made-up face, astounding me. 'Aarti, why don't you tell her what she should be doing on her golden night,' giggled Didi as she broke the ice between Aarti and me. Aarti stopped in her tracks, her face turned pale and she swallowed nervously. 'Didi, maybe we should tell her what not to do.'

The deafening silence that followed made me feel guilty. I wondered whether I had opened a Pandora's box that had led Aarti into the dark lanes of emotional and physical distress she never wanted to revisit. Aarti looked at me and began telling her story, 'My parents had always dreamt of a better life for us. A life that was "better" than the life we led in the village, bereft of luxuries. In my chosen life partner, his urban dwellings and "city boy" attitude were clear winners. None of us knew at the time that a life filled with love and respect is the true treasure that makes life worthwhile.'

She continued, 'I was perched upon his charpoy with a tall glass of milk, waiting for him to come to the room. Romantic songs from the movies of Shah Rukh Khan played in my head as I waited for him in eager anticipation, my heart fluttering, goosebumps on my arms. My reverie was broken by the loud slamming of the door. He entered staggering, shouting profanities at God knows who. He was drunk.'

'He pulled me into bed and ripped off my clothes. I was shocked and momentarily paralysed, he had just torn apart my mother's "shaadi ka joda", her gift to me. I was also scared and confused. I did not recognize this man in front of me, on top of me. He forced me into submission as I felt both physical and emotional pain. Little did I know at the time that I was being coerced, that I would be raped by my husband, every day, for the next seven years of my life and made to have three children.'

I couldn't stop myself from sobbing as Aarti paused for breath and a sip of water to gulp down her emotions. She was clearly distraught but still in control of herself, having accepted her reality. I learnt that Aarti and I were the same age and lived in the same city, but our lives couldn't have been more different. I was filled with a myriad of thoughts: 'Why did she not defend herself?', 'Why didn't she scream for help?', 'Why didn't she call the police?', 'Why didn't she kick him in the nuts?', 'Why, why, why?' After all, self-defence and being defiant have been the crusading symbols of the feminist movement portrayed through movies and other media we consume and have inevitably become the guiding light of today's woman.

Enraged at what I heard, I almost shouted, 'Aarti, but why did you have to suffer so much? Why did you not leave him?' Aarti smiled, a sad, humourless smile, as though berating me for my naiveté. 'It is not that easy to just leave a husband, not in my community. I did not want to become a disgrace to my parents,' she told me.

I was astounded by her response. But my judgement and personal bias crept in somewhere. I had set out as a researcher to unearth stories of family planning across the country. But this story had woken up the feminist in me. I wondered why it is still that difficult for a woman to make an independent decision despite having agency and a supportive family. Why must she live for everyone else first and for herself last, if at all? I had let my guard down and somewhere along the way Aarti became much more than just a research subject. My knowledge of her life led me to delve into my own life, to have a dialogue with myself, to consider my life's choices and the leap of faith I was about to take.

Didi took Aarti's hand in her own and clutched it tightly. 'Aarti's story is not one of a victim, it is that of a survivor,' she said. I felt comforted knowing that there was probably more to Aarti than met the eye.

'For seven years, I tried everything to turn around my husband's behaviour,' Aarti continued. 'I tried counselling, protection, alcohol rehab and many other things. The entire community knew of the sorry state of my marriage and tried to talk to my husband in their own way. Unfortunately, it was I who had to face his wrath each time someone offered him unsolicited advice. Finally, I knew this was it. After seven years of trying and failing, I knew he was not going to change. I also knew that if I wanted to survive and live, I had to think of something innovative. This is when Didi came into my life and told me that small things make a big difference. This was the turning point.'

'You both seem to be so tight, just like sisters,' I observed, smiling at them.

'We are more than sisters,' Aarti replied.

That's when it hit me – these two women were committed to each other. Their hearts and minds and souls dovetailed each other. Isn't that what a marriage is? Lost in my thoughts and the realization that I was witnessing something I was ill-prepared to understand, I lost my grip on the stainless steel glass of water I was holding. It crashed to the floor with a loud 'Ting!'

'Sorry, Didi. I don't know where I was lost. I will clean this up for you,' I offered. Ignoring me, they looked at each other. 'There couldn't be a better climax than the one we're about to tell you about,' Aarti winked.

'What do you mean, Aarti? Tell na!' I said.

'So you remember Didi had given me that advice that small things make a big difference?' said Aarti.

'Oh, yes!' I said.

'Then one night I had finally had enough. I was determined that I would not allow things to go the way they had been. Only I didn't know how to make it stop. Our bedroom door slammed open and my husband entered. As usual he was drunk out of his wits and could barely walk. I was hoping maybe he would collapse on the floor and fall asleep. But well, it's not that easy to tame monsters.'

'Aarti, weren't you scared? Please tell me you ran away from there,' I interjected, too anxious to wait to hear what happened next.

'Well, that night I decided to become the bigger monster,' said Aarti. 'He came up to me and pinned me to the charpoy. I got hold of a stainless steel glass that was within my reach. I thought I would hit him with it, hurt him, but as I lifted the glass to strike him, I had a better idea. I coyly took the glass and fit it between the ropes of the charpoy between my legs. My drunk husband was so out of his senses that he didn't realize he was doing it in a cup!'

'What?! How is that even possible,' I almost laughed.

'You see that's the difference between when you want to own someone and when you want to love someone,' Aarti explained, solemn and wise.

'What do you mean?' I asked puzzled.

'Every night he came into our room with a vengeance, his only thought was to put me in my place. Show me who the dominant one was in the relationship. He wanted to just let me know that he owned me and that I didn't have any autonomy over my own mind and body. With that mindset, when he had sex with me every night, he didn't care about pleasure, his or mine. Conquering and winning were all he had on his mind. Those 420 seconds at night gave him the feeling of ownership over me. But, finally, fighting back in my own way liberated me in more ways than one,' Aarti explained.

'Aarti, I still cannot believe how you came up with that solution. It's absolutely unthinkable,' I marvelled.

'I know, I too couldn't believe my own ingenuity,' she laughed. 'I tried this out several times over almost a year after that night and it miraculously worked each time. But every time I used my defence strategy, I knew sooner or later my cover would be blown. But until then it gave me some more time.'

'How did you gather the confidence to finally get rid of him? Please tell me that you're not with him any more?' The words were out of my mouth before I knew it.

'I am with him yet not with him.'

'What does that even mean?' I asked with a sense of urgency.

'I still adorn the symbols of a married woman – I wear my mangalsutra and put on my sindoor and bindi every morning. This is just so that I continue to get the *izzat* and the acceptance of a married woman in my society. The future of my kids is not questioned and I am not berated for being too bold. I have left his home and am now trying to carve out an independent life. I have even rented a small house for myself. My soul had detached from his a long time ago and now I am not physically tied to him any more either. If he ever shows up at my house drunk, I shoo him away. Let's just say that the Aarti of today stands more liberated than before, subjugated no more and to no one, unshackled by the physical and mental chains that had once clipped her wings,' she smiled.

'I hope your golden night is glitterier than mine. One, that you will find valuable and precious, a memory that you ought to reminisce with a smile on your face.'

Today I lead a golden life with my partner. A wedding is just a stamp that validates our vows to society and the law. Marriage is really about embracing one another and making each other's life golden, one night at a time.

Kopal's Takeaway

Aarti's story is a powerful reminder that true strength isn't always loud or visible – it's the quiet courage of surviving and reclaiming one's life. It's the courage to find freedom in the smallest of acts, even in the most broken moments. Aarti's journey shows that liberation isn't always a grand gesture; sometimes, it is a quiet rebellion against the forces that seek to diminish us. Her story shatters my heart, holding up a mirror to the uncomfortable truths of society that we often try to ignore. These stories matter because they remind us of the long road ahead – a battle we must continue to fight, no matter how hard it gets. And with each step, we grow stronger, united in our determination for change.

Story 3

The Stranger Who Proved Me Wrong About Trust

PRIYA MALIK

'Don't trust strangers.' It's something nearly every Indian child is taught from an early age. And it was no different for me. Growing up, I had heard this commandment so often that I rebelled at every chance I got and always tried to talk to strangers. Despite my apparent rebellion, the seed of doubt that had been sown too early and too deep within me had already germinated into a full-grown plant. Its fruit was a deeply bitter mistrust of strangers, which I tried my best to hide. After all, we were raised to be sceptical in a world full of deceit, lies and treachery. Distrusting the human race was a part of my self-preservation. And trust me, everything you read and see today will convince you why that was the perfect approach. However, being a travelling artist and an actor, I am required to travel to strange locations and deal with even stranger individuals and on occasion, trust these strangers.

Ironically, for someone who travels so much, going to an airport is an extremely stressful experience for me. I am envious of travellers who complete all formalities at the airport and then check into the lounge to post pictures of how much fun they are having as they sip their coffees and wines on their Instagram handles with #AirportDiaries. All those photos of runways and aeroplane flaps are the kind of things my nightmares are made of. No, actually, my airport nightmares begin way earlier – right at the check-in counter and persist like the burden of excess luggage until the very end of my journey.

My story begins with an event from several years ago. I had just travelled from Australia to India, with a Singapore layover, and finally landed in Mumbai. No sooner had I stepped out of the airport than I received a call informing me that I must begin the process of acquiring a US visa within the next twenty-four hours because that's where I would be travelling next with my theatre group. I was thrilled by the news but also terribly jet-lagged, barely able to keep my eyes open.

Despite the fatigue, I rested only for a few hours before arriving at the US embassy with my wallet, a small black purse filled with a lot of stress and jet lag. Finishing my paperwork, I set back for home in an Uber, looking forward to only one thing – a hot cup of chai. The only thing that I knew would help me at that moment. Then remembering I was out of milk, I requested my Uber driver to stop at my regular grocery store so I could pick up some milk. The taxi driver was kind and observant and asked me if I was doing okay because I appeared exhausted. I told him how I had just travelled from Australia and desperately needed a cup of chai. I quickly purchased the milk and then got dropped off at home.

I made my chai, drank it, went right back to bed and slept like a log for nearly twenty-four hours. Waking up the next morning, I felt refreshed and ready to face the day. So, I decided to do yoga. I made tea, packed my bag, changed my clothes and was ready to head to the yoga studio when I realized I couldn't find my small black wallet. This was not just any wallet; it contained about 500 Australian dollars, a pair of gold earrings, about 5,000–6,000 Indian rupees, all my credit and debit cards, IDs and, most importantly, my passport submission receipt. It was as if someone had pulled the rug from under my feet. I realized it had been over twenty-four hours since I last saw my wallet! Would I even manage to find it now? When did I last use it? I wondered, jogging my memory. Of course, at my local grocery shop, where I stopped for milk.

I called them right away, but they told me it wasn't with them. And, because they weren't strangers, I decided to trust them. I looked everywhere at home, and of course, it wasn't there either. That's when it struck me, perhaps I left it in the cab? Thankfully, I had my Uber driver's number in my call log, I dialled hoping he would answer. He answered immediately. 'Did I leave my wallet in your car?' I asked him. He replied, 'Arre madam, I've been waiting for your call since yesterday. Why did you call so late? I have your purse.' Stranger, danger. Punishment, reward. Many of my childhood lessons sped through my brain. I immediately hit the recording button on my phone. I asked him to come and return my wallet right away, promising him a reward of a thousand rupees if he did so immediately.

That's when he politely informed me, 'Madam, I can only come in the evening after finishing my work.' So, I decided to increase the reward amount. 'I'll pay you two thousand rupees, Bhaiya, please come now.' He laughed. 'I will but can only meet you in the evening.' Five thousand rupees?' 'Sorry, I really can't.' Finally, aware I couldn't do much at that moment, I agreed to wait for him until the evening.

Despite his promise, I couldn't get myself to trust him. So, I took all the precautions I could – I blocked all my cards and filed a lost item report with Uber. The only thing I didn't do was file a police report. That would be for later, I decided. Later in the evening, he called to inform me that he couldn't come to my place and requested that I meet him at Bandra station.

My trust in him was beginning to subside like the setting sun. Why did he change the plan? What was he 'planning'? Nevertheless, I agreed and told him to meet me outside Lucky Restaurant, even though I was feeling really unlucky at that moment. I took an auto to the station.

During the ride I was plagued by all kinds of evil thoughts. What if he didn't return my wallet? What if he demanded a larger reward? What if he assaulted me? What if he lured me into his taxi and took me elsewhere? The mantra 'Do not trust strangers' continued to echo in my ears on a loop like a broken record. By the time I arrived at 'Lucky' Restaurant, I was already feeling wary and threatened. Everything about the place made me suspicious, from the cobbler to the fruit vendor. What if they were all accomplices? What if someone was watching me? Maybe I shouldn't have come alone at all.

Suddenly, I saw someone smiling and waving at me from across the road. It was him. My Uber driver. He looked different, he was wearing a white kurta pyjama and a skullcap. It was Friday, *jumme ki raat*, and he was going to the mosque to offer his daily namaz. He walked up to me, my wallet in his hand. 'Here you go, Madam. Don't worry about it, it could have happened to anyone. Besides, you were very tired that day.'

I ignored his kindness, grabbing my wallet instead and opened it to check if something was missing. I couldn't believe that a stranger had kept my wallet for more than twenty-four hours and hadn't tampered with it at all. Everything was exactly as I had left it, except for the doubt that had taken over my mind. That had dissipated.

I offered him money as a reward, just like I had promised, but he refused it. I insisted and took out a few dollars, but he refused again. He had performed a good deed without any expectation of reward, which astounded me. How? I asked if he would like to eat something at the restaurant, but he politely declined, saying that it was time for his namaz. I then offered him a friendly cup of tea, hoping to give him some kind of reward, but he said something that stuck with me forever. He said, 'Madam, I haven't done this for any reward. I've done this for my faith.' Then he walked towards the mosque, leaving me standing there, alone, ashamed and with a valuable lesson learnt.

If this were a movie, the scene would have been extremely cinematic, with him walking away in slow motion while the azaan from the mosque slowly silenced my doubts. With my eyes closed, I sent up a silent prayer for him and left.

That day I learnt a very important lesson. I learnt that faith is the greatest reward one can receive. My Uber driver had taught me something much more valuable than my wallet. I realized that I would never teach my children to distrust strangers. Instead, I would teach them to gain the trust of others, just like my cab driver did. It is indeed the greatest reward we as humans can give one another.

Kopal's Takeaway

Your parents were right about strangers, but here's a story that tells why they were also *so* wrong. They told you never to trust strangers, and they weren't entirely wrong. But imagine a world where we all walk around with our earphones plugged in, shutting out every unfamiliar face and untold story. What kind of world would that be? A lifeless one. Real beauty lies in taking the leap of faith, in letting strangers leave their fingerprints on your life. Here's why trusting (even a little) might just make life extraordinary.

Story 4

I Am a Trans Woman and I Found My Soulmate

DANIELLA MENDONCA

From Daniel to Daniella; I have come a long way, and this story is my love letter to both of them.

When I was born, the doctors were unsure whether I was a boy or a girl and diagnosed me as intersex. An intersex person has reproductive or sexual anatomy that doesn't fit typical definitions of a male or a female. My karyotype was XXY. When my father found out, he rejected me at birth, calling me a 'chakka', but my mother stood by me, determined to raise me with love and care. After my father left us, we moved to the slums of Mumbai, where I grew up as Daniel, a boy.

As I grew older, I felt more connected with women. Everything about women, right from the way they dressed to the way they spoke – I felt comfortable around that energy. However, my mother was always concerned about societal acceptance and tried to protect me from the 'big bad world' by keeping me indoors.

That phase couldn't last long as I had to be sent to school; she put me in an all-boys school. It was the toughest phase of my life. The students would bully me, touch me inappropriately. Even the teachers made fun of me. When I told my Mom, she just consoled me and said, 'Koi baat nahi, beta, ek din sab theekh ho jayega tum dekhna.' (Don't worry, son, one day everything will be okay.)

I waited for that day, but things only got worse. One of the darkest phases of my life started when my cousin raped me when I was only in Grade 3. Heartbroken and shattered, I gathered the courage to tell my mother about this. Shocked, she decided to call my father after several years, and his response was, 'Achcha hai, abhi se seekh le, aadat dal lega. Kyuki aage jakar yehi toh hona hai.' (That's good, he must learn from now, because this will be his reality moving forward.)

As time passed, my mother and I were barely making ends meet; I was devastated to find that my mother was begging on the streets in order to send me to school. This became the turning point in my life. I decided to give into what everyone around me said I should be doing all along – become a sex worker. This phase of my life was all about figuring out a way to survive. From clapping at traffic signals during the day to selling my body for money at night, I did it all. I never felt small while doing any of these things, even though I was made to feel small every day. In a country like India, where the Hijra community is seen everywhere, on the streets, at traffic signals, in residential colonies, the lack of empathy and understanding for us is hard to comprehend.

It wasn't all bad though; one day while I was deboarding a train, I asked a lady to make space for me to get down. She was surprised by my good English and we got to talking. I told her how I used to go to school but couldn't any more. She offered to help me study and pass the Class 10 exam. I had rarely met anyone up until then in my life who was willing to see me beyond my gender identity. She saw me as human, and I decided to take a leap of faith with her.

Because of her, I managed to pass not only Class 10 but also Class 12 and ended up getting a degree in social work from Nirmala Niketan. This journey gave me so much confidence. I started seeing life beyond my miseries. In college, one of my teachers asked me to take part in a competition where I had to speak about myself; this was the first time I spoke about my journey and people had tears in their eyes. In that room, I felt love and acceptance from other people for the first time.

I know that my story so far sounds like the greatest tragedy of all time. But no, my story isn't meant to make you reach out for a tissue box. In fact, if I am grateful for anything in life, it's the hate I received early on in life. It made the victories sweeter than I thought. In 2024, I represented the United Nations LGBTQ+ community initiatives from India. Today, I hold a position on their advocacy council, where I provide guidance on creating inclusive spaces.

People often ask me when I 'came out' to the world. My response is always the same: I never came out; the only time I've 'come out' is from my mother's womb. I've always just been myself, living authentically without needing to make grand declarations.

In order to tell my real story, I had to give you this backstory. The story I want to tell today is one closest to my heart and I hope you will read it with an open mind and a full heart. Because it has the power to change your perspective.

So, while the whole world came to a standstill during COVID-19, things were moving at a very different pace for me. I had spent my entire life devoid of romantic relationships. In fact, even the thought of someone loving me, caring for me or wanting to spend their entire life with me sounded so alien that I barely thought about it.

Enter Joel.

I had befriended a boy named Joel and we got closer to each other especially when things got worse during COVID-19. I spent a lot of time with his family during the lockdown. I didn't even realize when I began to develop feelings for Joel. However, given my past, I could not confess my feelings for him, for I was scared of what the future would hold for a couple like us. To simply love someone seemed like the greatest act of rebellion at that point.

One day, I was cleaning vegetables at Joel's house when his mother asked me if I liked her son.

I was completely taken aback and, without even realizing it, blushed like a teenage girl and said yes. 'Do you like him the way a girl likes a boy?' she prodded. I couldn't look into her eyes at that moment but admitted, 'Yes, but please don't tell him. I fear it might ruin our friendship, especially since society doesn't even see me as a girl.'

What Joel's mother said next would be the one sentence that changed the trajectory of my life. 'When you see yourself as a girl in the mirror, you don't have to worry about society. You carry yourself with such grace, you are what you see yourself as when you look into the mirror.' She held my hand tight and gave me a look. A look that I can't put into words, but I think it said, 'I've already accepted you as my daughter-in-law.'

Days and months passed, and his parents started pulling my leg in front of him and teasing us jokingly. Once, we were travelling back from somewhere, and I gathered the courage to ask him, 'Doesn't it really matter or affect you when your parents pull my leg in front of you?'

He said, 'No, I actually like it.'

And that's how it all started.

Cut to his parents coming home to meet my mother. My heart was running at a billion-kilometre speed when they got talking about our marriage. I don't think my mother ever expected to see this day in her life. She only asked Joel one question: 'Do you have the courage to accept her the way she is in front of the whole society?'

To which Joel and his mother said yes, and that's how my happily ever after began. When most couples get married, they talk about their wedding attire or honeymoon destinations. We were having different conversations. We talked about how we would change people's minds when we got married, how we would handle the taunts and bullies and how we would show society that who we are and what we're doing is completely normal. I was ready to fight for love and ensure that our right to live authentically was recognized by this society.

Today, we are happily married. It's been two

years. Did you imagine my story would have a happy ending? Well, it did. I stand today as Daniella, a girl who has undergone a sex change surgery and is living her life on her own terms, wearing her favourite dresses, being with a man who stands by me and loves me deeply.

I had to go through a lot to get here and I continue to face several challenges every day. I am also fighting a larger battle – basic rights for our community, but I want to tell the world that there are all kinds of love in this world and that people should not have to justify their feelings to others. Every form of love is pure and must be accepted. Let's not love one another as a boy or girl, let's love each other as humans. If you see me as a human being, you'll see me for who I am, beyond my gender and who I choose to love.

Kopal's Takeaway

In a world that is torn apart every day with hate, Daniella's love acts like a soothing balm. If Daniella, despite all odds, could create the life she truly wanted, what's really stopping us? In her story, the unexpected hero, though, is her mother-in-law, Joel's mother – because the way she supports and nurtures their love is a true testament of how, sometimes, our greatest allies and sources of strength are right in front of us but we just don't recognize them. It's a reminder: the support you need, the love you crave, the life you're waiting for – it's all closer than you think.

Story 5

Why Do All These Slum Girls Dress Like Boys?

SALONI KAPOOR

For any Indian, Mumbai is the city of dreams. It's a place where people from all walks of life arrive with hope in their hearts and a twinkle in their eyes. However, the truth is that there are two Mumbais: one where dreams come true amid the glitz, glamour and red carpets, and the other in the massive slums covered by the quintessential blue plastic. We've heard enough stories from these slums, mostly of people who managed to cross over to the other side and made it big, but then there are the stories of those who stay, the ones we don't hear about.

This reality did not dawn upon me in my sheltered cocoon until I was exposed to the realities of slum living. As a volunteer with one of the leading community outreach organizations in India, I was part of the group that ran food distribution drives in the slum areas. Here, interactions with people led me to all kinds of experiences – some were wholesome, some threatening and some that tore my heart.

Among the many stories I heard and witnessed, there's one in particular that has stayed with me. This incident goes back to March 2015 when we were distributing food to children in the Marine Lines area. This area is located right next to a crowded and busy local train station. As we handed out food to some young boys, we asked them to form a line to ensure an efficient and organized distribution process. We have a sweet little custom we follow in every food drive we conduct. Before we start the distribution, we interact with the kids, ask them questions about their lives and school, and then start the distribution.

During this particular drive, while some of the volunteers were interacting with the kids, some of us went to fetch more food from the van. As I returned from the van carrying food packets in my hands, a fellow volunteer asked me if I had noticed something peculiar about these children. I was confused about what she was trying to say. As we approached the children, she said, 'Just take a closer look at them.'

It was then that we realized that despite their appearance, they weren't all boys. When we asked them their names, they responded with names like Rajeshwari and Suneeta. They all had short hair, almost identical, and were dressed in what seemed like boys' clothing. If you didn't look very closely, you wouldn't be able to tell that they were girls. We were taken aback, as it wasn't just one of them looking like a tomboy; all of them had a distinctive boyish appearance.

I asked one of the volunteers, 'Why do these little girls look like boys?' She approached a woman sitting near a hut where we were serving food. We enquired about why these little girls were dressed like boys, and her response was something none of us were prepared for.

She told us how these girls were born in this slum, and have always lived together as a group. Their parents have always cared for them and loved them deeply. However, they mostly work as labourers and their work timings can be ridiculous, leaving really early in the morning and returning late. In their absence, one day, one of the little girls was sexually assaulted. The perpetrator took her away, and she was never seen again. To prevent such incidents, their parents started disguising these girls as boys, concealing their true identity for safety reasons.

How had we not considered how rough their lives on the street could be? We couldn't know this and not do something about it.

We collectively brainstormed ways to prevent such tragedies from recurring in the future. Our aim was to help these girls feel comfortable and secure in their own identities, without the need to disguise themselves as boys to avoid threats on the streets.

This experience was a wake-up call during my initial months of volunteering. I realized that while we provided food to these children, we left with valuable insights into their lives, perspectives, emotions and the daily challenges they faced. Living on the streets exposed them to dangers we couldn't fully comprehend because of our sheltered lives. After learning about these girls, we decided to take action to protect them and empower them to live without the fear of abduction or sexual assault.

We began to arrange for judo and karate lessons to teach them self-defence. We educated them about the buddy system, ensuring they were always with a companion. One of our volunteers even guided them to the local police station, as they were unaware of how close it was and we encouraged them to report any incidents promptly. We continued visiting this area for several weeks to check on their progress. One day, we visited the slum and were welcomed with the sweetest smiles we had ever seen.

I was teary-eyed to see two of the girls had grown their hair and were wearing dresses. One of them approached me and said, 'Didi, we want to look like you,' referring to the volunteers.

That moment felt surreal.

I deeply wished that no child would ever have to live in such fear and that no girl would have to hide her identity for any reason. I hoped that these young girls would develop their own identities, free from the need to pretend to be someone else. Seeing them play together, dressed in cute little dresses, their hair flying in the breeze, is an image I will always hold close to my heart. While it might seem ordinary to most, to me it represents a childhood lived beyond the tragedies of society.

Kopal's Takeaway

Saloni's story holds a special place in my heart – it was one of the first few stories we uploaded to Tape A Tale's website in audio format. I've lived with this story for seven years and yet, every time I revisit it, it strikes a chord as deeply as it did the first time. It's so crucial for us to get involved in whatever capacity we can to make a difference. There is always room to a do a little for the people around you. Take this story as your call to action.

Story 6

How I Overcame Tragedy and Won Gold for India

EKTA BHYAN

I'll start my story with three truths and no lies.

I have won a gold medal for India in sports.

I am in a wheelchair.

One day and one decision can make or break your life.

We often think that we have a plan for life, but the truth is that, more often than not, life has a plan for us. This, however, doesn't mean that we don't have control over things, it only means that our story, our life, and our legacy are about what we make out of that plan.

In 2003, I found myself in the grip of such a moment, where all of a sudden, life put me at a crossroads that would forever change my life. But before I share that story, let me take a step back. I was born in 1985 in Hissar, Haryana, and I was the second child among my siblings. My life was quite simple – I was a diligent and studious young girl. Due to my deep love for academics, it was clear to me that my career path would lead me to do something worthwhile, something my family and I could be truly proud of. Whenever someone asked me what I wanted to be when I grew up, I would happily respond, 'A doctor.' With this dream firmly set in my mind, I completed my Grade 12 exams in 2003 and with the sole purpose of excelling in the medical entrance exams, I enrolled in a coaching centre.

It was the very first day of my coaching when fate chose to intervene. On my way to the coaching centre, I met with an accident. My spine broke but what I didn't realize at that moment was that it was truly my dreams that were broken. I had to undergo several surgeries. Once the initial chaos was over, the doctors broke the news to us – one that would change my life forever: I had a spinal cord injury that had paralysed my legs. As I lay on that hospital bed, the world as I knew it ceased to exist. My dreams of becoming a doctor, of making my family proud, of living an independent life, were crushed in that collision.

The agony of helplessness gnawed at me. At first I thought I'd be able to walk on my own but after spending nine months of my life on the hospital bed, I realized I would never be able to walk on my own. This broke me and my dreams. Life meant nothing to me at that time. While my peers were pursuing their dreams, I was still there on the hospital bed, struggling to even stand on my legs.

But that's the thing about life, it just keeps on moving even when your entire world comes to a standstill. While my future appeared bleak, like a big black cloud, my parents had to think about the inevitable 'What next?' They made a courageous decision for my future at a time when I had no idea what lay ahead. They enrolled me in a respected college to pursue a degree in English honours, supporting me to complete my graduation. It wasn't easy for me to navigate a new college in a wheelchair. Numerous questions flooded my mind. Everyone would stare, as though I didn't belong there, as though I was out of place. I could see the sympathy in most eyes, and I despised it.

People typically associate wheelchairs with the elderly, yet I was very young – only 18 when the accident occurred. They would say, 'It's so disheartening to see someone so young leading such a challenging life.' These words affected me, but they couldn't shatter my confidence.

One day, while attending a lecture in college, our strict professor posed a question that stumped my classmates. I raised my hand and provided the correct answer. He beamed with pride and said, 'One day, this girl will do wonders; she'll reach for the sky.' After my accident, this was the first time I had heard someone say something so positive about me.

It boosted my confidence, and in my first year, I topped my college in psychology, which was one of the subjects I had opted for in my course. Here was another boost for my confidence, and I began preparing for other exams. I was selected as an auditor and then an English postgraduate teacher by the Haryana government. In 2013, I successfully cleared the state civil service examination and was appointed as an assistant employment officer. I realized that I might be physically disabled, but my grit, my perseverance and my dreams were all still thriving.

I now had a great government job, and my family was happy. Yet, despite the achievements and the contentment this job brought to my family, I hungered for more. I knew I was meant for something greater. While in college, a teacher once told me that there's always room for improvement, and I've lived by that mantra ever since.

I yearned to do something more significant, something bigger. When I cleared the state civil service examination, my interview was published in the newspaper, and it was through that that I met Amit Saroha, a Paralympian. My journey towards a deeper purpose took an unexpected turn when I crossed paths with him. His story and spirit ignited a newfound passion within me for para athletics, a path I had never previously considered. This decision wasn't easy for me, but I wanted to prove to myself that I was limitless. So, inspired by his words, I dared to challenge my physical limitations.

I began training under him for club throw and discus throw. It was the first time I had engaged in any physical activity since my accident. I practised for three hours in the morning and three hours in the evening. I put in all my effort, and my hard work paid off when I participated in the National Para Athletics Championship held in Panchkula, where I won my first gold medal in club throw and a bronze medal in discus throw. After that, there was no looking back. Then I was selected for the 2016 IPC Grand Prix held in Berlin, where I won the silver medal in club throw. I continued competing in nationals and won medals in consecutive years. Each medal I held in my hands provided me with a resurgence of power. I craved more, and that insatiable desire drove me to compete on even bigger platforms. I always yearned for 'more', which led me to compete in the World Para Athletics Championship in 2017. I was ranked first in Asia in club throw and sixth in the world. All of this was just the beginning. Despite a setback at the 2020 Paralympics, I remained undeterred and won a gold medal at the World Championships in 2024.

For a girl who once believed her life had been determined by her accident and that she was destined to spend a sub-ordinary existence in a wheelchair, this journey meant everything. Looking back, I wish I could tell that young girl to take a deep breath; life has a way of unfolding beautifully, even in the face of adversity.

I know it's very tough for people like me. At first, I thought it was just me, that I was the only one whose life was challenging. But when I met other para athletes, I realized that barriers and struggles are universal, and disability, in all its forms, exacts a steep cost.

Disability is a costly thing, physically, mentally and financially, but trust me, it's not the end. You are limitless; you just need to realize your potential and never stop believing in yourself. Life may hand us lemons, but it's our choice to transform them into refreshing lemonade and savour the sweetness of life.

Kopal's Takeaway

You need to show up every day, in every way, because consistency is where growth begins. Show up for your goals with small steps. Even on hard days, showing up is how you build the life you want.

Story 7

The Last Gift My Brother Left Me

SHWETA SHARMA

'What kind of shirt are you wearing? It's so loose! I don't know what you people do in the name of fashion!'

'Oh Mom, this is what we call a baggy style. It's meant to be loose-fitting. Mom, comfort is in fashion now. You won't understand, right?'

'But don't you have your own clothes? Why do you have to wear your brother's?'

My brother is two years older than me. Our family? The picture-perfect, typical Indian one with two sweet children. Whether you call it the classic Indian sibling dynamic or the Tom and Jerry show, there wasn't much difference. Even on the most perfect days, we always managed to find a reason to fight, smack each other on the head or argue over the smallest things. We were so different in every way that no conversation ever ended without there being some sort of argument or disagreement.

He had Honey Singh's rap songs on his playlist, while I preferred Bhupinder Singh's soulful tunes. We would often fight over the remote or argue about who got more Maggi. Like any siblings, my brother and I have shared it all – playing together, studying together, sipping Rasna on hot summer days, or watching *Tarak Mehta ka Ooltah Chashmah* while snacking. We did everything together.

After completing Class 12, my brother decided to study engineering. Suddenly, our seventeen-year relationship was about to turn into a long-distance one. We both knew that long-distance never works. But as they say, sometimes you have to leave where you are to get to where you're meant to be. So, what happened next was inevitable. Dad's money was flowing, and our shopping sprees began – new clothes, new shoes, a shiny new trolley. Everything was fresh, just like the new chapter in my brother's life. The eldest son of the house was going to live alone for the first time. It was a bittersweet moment, filled with joy and pride for all of us.

He was leaving for another city and, oddly enough, I was happy about it. Finally, the TV remote would be mine. The entire room would be mine. Only my secrets would fill the space. Then, the day arrived. He woke up at 7 a.m., ready to head to the airport. No matter how much we used to fight or how many times I claimed I wouldn't miss him and couldn't wait for him to leave, deep down I knew I'd miss him terribly. But in a middle-class family you just don't say things like 'I'll miss you' or 'I love you' to your sibling. It's just not something you do, right?

I wanted to hug him. I wanted to hold him so tightly that he couldn't leave. I wanted to say, 'Keep the TV remote. Let your playlist play. Just stay.' But I couldn't. I stood there, watching him walk down the stairs, and as he did, tears rolled down my cheeks. My heart felt like it was sinking. I quickly wiped them away, forcing myself to hold it together. He reached the door and turned to me. 'Don't cry, no hugs,' he said, grinning. 'My clothes will get ruined. I'm not going away forever, am I?'

A few months later, the lockdown brought him back home. All the colleges shut down, and our daily battles over the remote resumed. Other familiar routines followed – me doing his work and pitching him business ideas over momos. Everything felt like it was back to normal. But life, as always, had its own plans.

Cut to 27 August 2021.

I was woken up by my mom's panic-filled voice.

'Tell him to open the door. He has been sitting inside the room for so long. I have work, and he's not even answering the phone.'

Why wasn't he answering the phone? I went up to the door and started knocking loudly,

'Enough with the jokes, open the door, buddy. I'll treat you to momos.'

Normally, my brother would come out as soon as he heard there were momos, but that day he didn't. We knocked on the door for a long time. No response. I peeped through the keyhole and looked into the room. Until that moment, I had only heard the phrase 'the ground slipped from under my feet' but that day I felt it. I felt it the moment I saw my brother hanging from the ceiling.

After that, everything was a blur. I don't remember anything, or perhaps I don't want to recall. What I do remember is women crying around me. I remember women shouting. I remember people rushing to the hospital. I remember his cold body.

Our long-distance relationship was meant to be a temporary phase. But now, he was gone forever. He'd promised to buy me an iPhone. Now, he'd never fulfil that promise or any of the others he'd made to me. He couldn't because he was gone. Dead. By suicide. He took his own life. And in doing so he took away a part of me, and everything my family held on to. Everything. He was gone, just like that. Why? No one knows. I felt broken. Betrayed.

He had left, but I remained. Stuck in that moment. Even today, here I am, still stuck in that moment.

I keep wondering, despite spending so much time with my brother, I did not know what he was going through. He is gone but the pain he felt will live within all of us, forever. I wish people would speak more about their mental health, I wish we learn to see things beyond what our eyes can see. I wish we could create a safe space around us for our loved ones to tell us when they need help. I wish…

It has been nearly two years since the incident. I have celebrated my first birthday, my first Holi, my first Diwali without him. Time doesn't stop for anyone. It keeps flowing and takes you along with it.

People think I've moved on, and honestly, I try hard. I questioned my love for him, I tried hating him for his actions. But you can't hate someone you love, even if they break your heart. I spent a lot of time and tried everything, but couldn't move on. It took time, but I realized that's the thing – I don't want to move on. This pain will stay with me, because it is the one thing that even today connects me to my brother. I know many people out there have gone through this pain, and some are still healing. I want you to know that it's going to be fine. They're with you, they're within you. Find them, in their books, in the melodies of their favourite songs, within yourself. I know it's tough but hold on to your pain. Sometimes feeling the wounds can lessen them.

Now I've moved to Delhi. Whenever I miss home, I make his favourite coffee and watch *Veer-Zaara*. Whenever I miss home, I take out his shirt, iron it and wear it. Mom doesn't like me keeping his clothes safe like this. She says I won't be able to move on.

'Oh Mom, these loose clothes are in fashion. You won't understand.'

Who will make her understand? It's not just about comfort or fashion. It never was.

Kopal's Takeaway

I often wonder, if we lived in a world where talking about mental health wasn't stigmatized or dismissed, would we still hear stories like Shweta's? What if help was as easily accessible for emotional pain as it is for a fever – something that no one questions? I wish we could speak more openly about mental health with the same understanding and empathy we offer for physical ailments. If you or someone you know is struggling, please reach out to a professional for help. I hope Shweta's story and her vulnerability will provide someone the strength they need. I truly believe it will.

Story 8

If Karma Exists ... Is It Always a 'Bitch'?

RASHMI KURUP

What you sow, you reap; the concept of karma is as simple as that. However, the twist comes when what you are sowing is almost always something negative. The word karma is often used to deter action by implying that if you do something wrong, you'll face bitter consequences. But the real question is: Why does everyone only refer to karma in relation to evil?

Whenever a friend lets us down, or a relationship falters, we often say, 'They did me wrong, karma will get them.' Recently, when I lost my favourite book, my friend called it 'instant karma' because I had refused to lend it to her the previous day. Is that what karma means? Tit for tat? Punishment?

On 26 July 2006, the day when Mumbai came to a standstill, I encountered the real face of Karma. Thousands of people were stranded on the flooded streets. A lot of them had lost their livelihoods and many had lost their lives. There was no transportation, no electricity, no communication. While our beautiful chaotic city drowned, my mom and I feared the worst while sitting in our completely dry home. My father had been missing for three days. He hadn't come home and hadn't contacted us either. As I stood on my terrace, looking around, I felt as though I was on an island – all around me houses had been submerged in water, the neighbourhood I lived in was nearly gone. Amidst all this, the fear of 'what ifs' clouded both our minds.

Fortunately, the water hadn't got into our housing complex, and so it turned into a temporary shelter for many who were stranded or had lost their own homes. I had just stepped out of the bathroom when I saw two kids in our living room. I had never seen them before.

My mother was busy talking to a woman who could only have been their mother. Wait. Those kids were wearing my clothes. My brand-new clothes. I marched into the living room and glared at my mother. She caught the dark look on my face and took me to the bedroom before I could say anything. 'Those are my clothes you've given away to two random kids! I have not worn them even once. My birthday dress, Amma. They might not even return it! We don't even know them! Why don't you give them some worn-out clothes?'

The look on her face, however, silenced me. The words she spoke in that moment are etched so deep in my mind that I remember them even today. 'They deserve better than your old clothes. They are going through a very tough phase in their lives right now. It is our duty to help them. It doesn't matter if they don't return your new clothes. Some day when you really need it, this good karma will come back to you in some form.'

At that moment, I couldn't fathom what she was saying. All I could see was my birthday dress on a stranger. I wished so hard at that moment that my father was there; I wished he hadn't left the house for office the other day. Everything would have been normal today. I knew, however, that throwing a fit in that moment wasn't something my already worried mother would entertain, so I let it pass. I hadn't forgiven Amma for her actions though.

By evening, the water in our area began to recede. The family camping in our living room left, hoping to make their way through the flood. That same evening I opened the door to find my father standing in front of me. Drenched to the skin, exhausted beyond words, haggard and hungry, but alive. I had never been so happy to see him; I jumped to hug him.

Later that evening, as I served him food, he began to narrate the horrors he had witnessed in the last three days – of a mighty city brought to its knees by the waters. He told us how he had hired a cab from his office to the railway station but had been stuck in traffic for nearly six hours. Fortunately, a co-passenger and he spent the time together, strangers-in-arms, supporting each other when their dear ones couldn't. Then, tired of waiting, they started walking towards home. By the time it was dark, the water in most places was almost waist-high. The man he had been walking with reached his home and offered Dad shelter for the night. This man's small 1-BHK flat became my father's refuge for the next two days. But it wasn't Dad alone living there; they had opened their house to many others like him – stranded men and women – and they had even shared their food. My dad owed his life to the man whose new shirt he wore on his way back home.

I was stunned to hear this story. At night as I stared sleeplessly at the ceiling, my mom, who was lying next to me, whispered into my ear, 'Would you have liked it if your dad was offered old worn-out clothes instead?'

karma is not a bitch, but the most beautiful lesson life can teach you. Fortunately for me, I learnt the true meaning of karma very early in life. Even after twenty years, every moment of that day remains etched in my memory. While not everyone witnesses the results of karma as instantly as I did, there is something profoundly poetic about knowing that what you put into the universe comes back to you – not necessarily in the same shape and form, but always similar in essence.

Kopal's Takeaway

A beautiful, poetic tale about a mother teaching her daughter the real meaning of Karma. This story comes as a gentle reminder that the universe is always listening and expanding in the direction we want through our actions. It is a reminder to be kind in our actions. It will reward us in surprising ways.

Story 9

How I Fought Back After My Husband Threw Acid on Me

MEENA SONI

One moment in my life changed everything, but if there's anything you take away from my story, let it be the courage and strength with which I rebuilt my life after that moment. The moment itself isn't what defines me – it's the resilience that followed, which is the true heart of my story.

I am Meena Soni. I belong to a small village near Lucknow. I am a mother of three, and I was married when I was very young. My husband was a jewellery artisan; but soon after my marriage he quit work as he was diagnosed with tuberculosis (TB).

I knew I had to feed my children and give them a better life. And so I became the breadwinner and started working at a women's organization as their project manager, but the wages were low; only I know how I managed at that time.

My husband and in-laws were not quite happy with the fact that I was earning money. There was this one time when my husband gave me the choice to either continue working or leave his house. I chose to leave. A few years later, my husband came to me and expressed his desire to patch up and we started living together. I thought there might have been a change of heart and agreed without realizing his real intentions.

Even after three children and going through so much, I don't know what got into his head – he accused me of cheating just because I came home late from work. I tried my best to make him understand that it wasn't the case and that it wasn't in my control, as we had deadlines and we worked accordingly. I had a clear vision in my head – I knew that I had to work hard because I had a family to support.

Then, I started working as a reporter for a local newspaper called *Khabar Lahariya*. My schedule was unstable, and I would usually leave home by six in the morning and return only by 8 p.m. This triggered my husband more, and what had earlier been a mere doubt in his mind turned into solid belief. As a result, we began to have arguments, and that created differences between us.

It was the summer of 2004. I had an off from the office, and I had no idea what my husband was planning. While I was sleeping, my husband threw acid at me, waking me up in the most cruel, painful way imaginable. I ran out of the house screaming in pain and my husband caught hold of my saree, and tried to kill me. I threw my saree away and ran to escape. I asked my daughter to call a rickshaw to take me to the doctor.

By this time, a large crowd had gathered outside my house, but not a single person came forward to help me. I was wearing only a petticoat and blouse, yet not a single person offered to help me.

As a society, they failed me. We have so many opinions and impositions for how women should dress and behave, but the same society couldn't be bothered to provide me with anything to cover my body. That day, I went to the hospital alone. I don't know where I got the strength from but it overpowered my entire being.

Thankfully, the doctor I went to was the same person whom I had interviewed a day before for the newspaper. He recognized me and started my treatment right away. While I was being treated I learnt that my husband had tried to die by suicide, and we both were shifted to a hospital in Allahabad. He died on the fifth day. For me, he was dead the day he threw acid on me.

I was in the hospital for about three months. My children went to live with my in-laws. The NGOs that I worked with supported me in all possible ways. They got me all the medical assistance I needed. Finally, I was back, but in a different shape. The Meena Soni I am today is so different from the Meena Soni I used to be.

My face was horribly scarred and I couldn't bear to look at myself in the mirror. I stayed away from my children for months as I was worried that if they looked at me, they would get scared and not come to me. When I was discharged, I realized I was back to square one, and it was even worse than before. Previously, I could interact with people to earn a living, but now, with this face, no one would wish to be near me, let alone talk to me. I couldn't continue working at *Khabar Lahariya*. All I got from most of the people was sympathy, but that was not what I was looking for. I needed work.

So, I gathered my courage and contacted Madhavi didi from Sanatkada Samajik Pahel, with whom I used to work before becoming a reporter. She gave me the strength I needed to stand up for myself after everything I had been through. She told me I could still do things for myself, and it was about time I did.

So, I joined her NGO and made a promise to myself that I wouldn't let any woman suffer the pain I had endured. I would fight for them and do everything within my means to help them.

Being a woman and living in a male-dominated society, things were never easy but I didn't give up.

Today I work for undertrial women in jails and get them legal assistance. I have got forty of them out on bail. We also provide them with skill-based training so they can stand on their own feet once out of jail. Whatever happened to me only made me stronger. It taught me the importance of self-belief and never giving up, even in the face of overwhelming challenges. I also work with acid attack survivors and help them rebuild their lives.

I have and will always remain committed to my cause of working for women and with women victims and giving them the courage to stand up for themselves. I want my children to be independent and make a difference in society as well. Today people know me for the work I have done; I can look at the mirror and feel proud about how I learnt to love myself for my scars. How they now remind me of my strength and resilience. Do I miss the old me? I do but the new me has a story to tell; a story that I want every woman looking into the mirror and questioning her self-worth to hear.

Kopal's Takeaway

I've had the privilege of knowing Meena Ma'am for years – ever since my days at Sanatkada as an intern, which I mention in the introduction of this book. Her story is one that never fails to give me goosebumps. She has empowered me countless times by simply living her truth. She rewrote her life, word by word, going from strength to strength. Her story is a solid reminder that, in the end, you have to pick yourself up and rebuild your own life. No one else can do that for you.

Story 10

How Blindness Led Me to Conquer Mountains

MANDAVI GARG

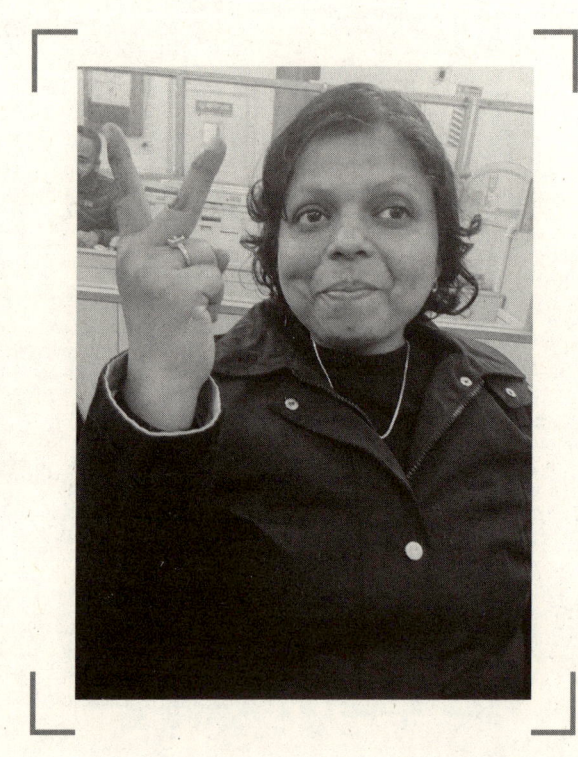

I was the kind of kid who always had cotton and Betadine ready for when I came back from playing outside. I was that rough-and-tumble, outdoorsy child. I remember playing cricket with the boys, cycling without touching the handles and doing my own stunts, especially during the heavy winter fog. You're probably starting to see why cotton and Betadine were my best friends. Little did I know, though, that by the time I turned six, all my summers, springs and autumns would start getting foggy too. I was going blind.

I wish there was a Harry Potter spell for this, but no, the reality is that I have retinitis pigmentosa – a retinal disorder that causes gradual, unpredictable and irreversible loss of eyesight. My father has it too; it's hereditary. He was able to see my brother's face, but he never got to see mine. Still, I'm grateful that I got to see him. Back in school, I used to be a last bencher, but each year, I kept moving closer to the front until, by the time I reached Grade 8, I couldn't even read from the first row.

In Grade 10, when our board exam centres were in different schools, it became a nightmare for me. I once asked the teachers there for extra light, but since they did not understand my condition, instead of understanding and accommodating me, they said things like, 'She might have plans to cheat.'

What makes me even sadder is that I used to play judo and had almost gotten selected in the Atlanta Olympics too, but I could never chase that dream because none of that mattered, because from where I come from, studies are everything. But I did find some solace in my favourite subject, accounts.

I loved that subject and was really great at it – so much so that other kids would come to me with their queries. But it was extremely demanding on my eyes. I had hoped to pursue commerce in Ahmedabad, but instead I opted for arts and chose psychology. Throughout this time, I faced several minor physical accidents, and by the final year of my bachelor's degree, I had completely lost my independence. I couldn't even walk without someone's assistance, and I genuinely didn't know what to do with my life.

Around that time in 2005, when my brother got married, my sister-in-law started searching for courses for the blind on Google. She helped me change the trajectory of my life. We found an institute in Delhi where I enrolled in a computer course.

For over a month, one of the volunteers there thought I was also dumb and deaf, and honestly, I don't blame her. I had become that person who wouldn't speak or react. I felt like I couldn't stand in front of anyone, like I was nothing, no one.

Working on the computer course did help boost my confidence. Eventually, I was also assigned to travel from Hauz Khas to RK Puram by the director there to help gain confidence to travel alone. She worked extensively with me on mobility and provided counselling to help me with my overall mental wellbeing. The first few times she would let go of my hand during tasks, I would faint. I would become so overwhelmed that instead of taking a step, the whole world would start spinning, and I would collapse. But slowly and gradually, I made progress. However, it wasn't easy.

After six months at the blind institute, I began speaking with other blind individuals at the centre. It was around this time that I met Manvendra, the captain of the blind cricket team for three World Cups. He was partially blind and eight years older than me. Meeting him felt like a breath of fresh air. Despite the hardships in his life, he remained so full of life, always ready to help a friend, give advice, or lend a shoulder to cry on.

He kept reminding me, 'Just because one thing is gone doesn't mean you have to let go of everything else.' It felt like I had found an elder brother. He noticed how I had given up on so many of my dreams and how I had let my studies take a back seat. Manvendra encouraged me to continue pursuing my dreams, reminding me that we now have the technology to support us. He suggested that I pursue higher studies and helped with the process too.

In 2006, I applied to Delhi University and Jamia Millia Islamia (JMI) and secured admission. The competitor in me was ready, and I was faring well academically. However, by the time I reached my final year, I stumbled once again, this time with my confidence.

Until then, I could see the pillars in my hostel, which helped me navigate my way, but slowly I lost that vision too. There wasn't a day when I didn't fall or run into a wall. The kind of embarrassment I felt was mortifying. I would have easily been selected for campus recruitment interviews, but whenever they discussed field placements, I would get cold feet. I did manage to get a job with a salary of ₹10,000 a month, while everyone else received packages of ₹30,000 to ₹40,000.

The company promised ₹10,000 but said only ₹5,000 would be mine – the rest was for the cab. Things got worse when they stopped providing the cab after two weeks, leaving me to rely on Noida's chaotic buses in 2008. One day, the bus changed its route, and I was forced to get off. That day, I didn't even have my stick. Lost and overwhelmed, I asked for help, but people ignored me.

I had the worst day of my life trying to get home. After that, I was done. I stayed in my room for months. I didn't know what to do with my life. A girl who had always lived life to the fullest had forgotten what it was like to even smile. I was tired of being dragged back to zero by life again and again. I had forgotten what my dreams were. Due to a lack of finances, I took up another job in the banking sector.

Just when I thought this was what the rest of my life would look like, I happened to attend a meeting in Delhi focused on technology for the blind, where I met Atul Sir, a senior manager at the Tata Steel Adventure Foundation, led by Bachendri Pal. Even Premlata Agrawal, the first woman to scale the Seven Summits, was present there.

In my conversation with him, I told Atul Sir about my love for sports and how much I enjoyed exploring as a child. Without hesitation, Atul Sir asked me, 'What's stopping you now?' He said, 'You can still do it.' He told me about mountaineering and how he had climbed more than 10,000 feet, and he offered to arrange a trek for me. His voice sounded like the most bittersweet melody I had ever heard. I didn't know what to say; I couldn't believe it was even possible.

'What's stopping you now?' I asked myself again and again, and I didn't have an answer.

I went on a trek in Himachal Pradesh along with a group of blind individuals. Some of these people had summited mountains. The moment I completed this trek, my life changed 180 degrees.

A year later, Bachendri Ma'am, who had led the first trek, asked me if I would want to summit Mount Kanamo, which is 19,600 feet (the seven highest continental peak in the world). I asked her, 'Ma'am, will I be able to do it?'

She replied, 'How would I know? Now tell me, are you coming or not?'

I said, 'Yes. I am.'

On the day of the final summit, we were told that our tea would be ready by 3 a.m. because we needed to return as soon as possible due to the unfavourable weather. However, that morning, I woke up with body pain and fever. I considered giving up, just like the others, but I hadn't come this far to quit. So, I took some medicine and after three hours, I somehow managed to reach the summit. I felt invincible. On our way back, I met Bachendri Ma'am, who hadn't accompanied us to the final part of the summit. She was waving at me, screaming with joy. 'Yes! Mandavi! You did it! You are the first blind woman to have ever scaled this mountain.' Tears rolled down my cheeks. I didn't even know what I had signed up for, but she did. It felt like the little Mandavi who spent all her time outdoors playing sports had come to life again. My childhood didn't feel like a distant memory at that moment.

Since then, I have completed a mountaineering course at the Nehru Institute of Mountaineering, successfully climbed Kang Yatse, cycled 350 kilometres from Ahmedabad to Junagadh, and achieved much more. My life has felt like a massive, turbulent journey, but I have finally reached where I was meant to be.

After all these years, it feels like the cotton and Betadine can again wait for me at home. I am still that girl. I understand that people often assume I am struggling to survive because I am blind, but that isn't the case with me. I want to be remembered as the girl who nearly got lost in the dark but never gave up on the light. Today, I don't sit and regret the bad cards that fate dealt me, rather I feel proud of being able to live a full life, and carving my own destiny.

Kopal's Takeaway

Hope is always within reach, especially when we need it most. Find it within you, around you.

Story 11

———•———

The Day My Great-Grandmother Chose to Die – Then Lived

MAHITHA

Front row (left to right): Mom, Great-Grandmother, Krishnamma (Kitakammachi), Grandmother, Janaki
Back row: Mahitha (left) with cousins and niece

My great-grandmother was 90 the summer she decided she was going to die.

We children always spent our holidays with our grandparents, and we happened to be in our maternal grandmother's home where our grandmother's mother, Kitakammachi, as we called her, also lived. It was our last day of holiday, when Kitakammachi slipped in the bathroom.

Even though she proved to be tougher than the rough cement floor, she decided her time was up, and that she was going to speed up the process by giving up food first, then water. The family gathered to sit by her bed.

Friends and relatives heard she was unwell, and wasn't eating, and they came to sit by her, sombre-faced, saying their goodbyes. Her food on earth is over, the older people said knowingly. The younger people sipped tea and exchanged gossip.

Six days passed. Her deep baritone that could rattle the rafters softened. Slightly.

That's all. As far as anyone could see, she wasn't going anywhere.

We teased her that even Yama Dharmaraja (God of Death) was too afraid to come for her.

Krishnamma, or Kitakammachi (combination of her nickname and her word grandmother) – big-bosomed, skin criss-crossed with countless lines, fingers always busy – was a woman with a soft heart and a loud voice; a feminist in spirit long before the word came into common parlance.

Her love for her great-grandchildren was pure, untainted gender or skin colour biases, and she was as fiercely protective of us as she was of the *sapotas* (chikoo) growing in her front yard.

'Ey, daaktaroo!' she would shout out to the village doctor who visited her once a week.

'Don't even think about touching the fruit, they are for the children when they come to visit me!' He would quickly jerk his hand back, pretending he was just reaching out to scratch his head and scurry away.

By day seven, eating nothing, taking only a sip of water when my mother or a visiting relative berated her, reduced to little more than bones draped with folds of skin as dark as the blistering pepper mutton she made once in a rare while, covered with a piece of coarse white cotton cloth. She spoke only to demand a bedpan, to shush our irreverent giggly comments when we girls took turns to wipe her down or to exclaim in wonder at the scented soap we used – she had used only plain gram flour from when she was 15 years old, as befitted her status as a widow.

On day eight, a cousin sent home a basket of the sweetest, juiciest kudhadath mangoes. 'Give me a slice,' she demanded. Thrilled that she had finally showed interest in food, we cut her some. 'Oh, look at her,' my grandmother remarked sarcastically. 'Mangoes from *her* farm, and suddenly she doesn't want to go to heaven any more!'

Her farm? Wasn't Kitakkammachi a widow with no material assets? 'Yes,' Amma said. 'Her farm. She had once owned lands all the way from Mettupalayam to Coimbatore.' Hmmm … We didn't know that. We did know though that Kitakammachi loved jewellery. She would trace our noses and the curve of our ears and tell us about the different kinds of ornaments she used to wear; the necklaces in varying lengths, the oddiyanams, the nath, the bullak, the besari and so many different kinds of earrings; she even had the cartilage and tops of her ears pierced!

'I still remember when I got my piercing,' she would tell us, pulling on the little triangle of flesh to display the mark. 'It made a "ppadakk" sound, and it hurt for one whole week.'

'Did you cry, Ammachi?'

'No, why would I? I wanted to do it, and it was worth the pain.' She would urge us to wear nose pins and septum rings, and we would laugh at the thought of sporting such unfashionable jewellery.

Kitakkammachi was her father's favourite. And her love for jewellery was well known. So, along with the lands stretching all the way from Mettupalayam to Coimbatore, Kitakkammachi also received huge quantities of jewellery. 'Platters, and platters,' she would say, and shrug when we asked what happened to it. All of it was lost when she lost her husband, we heard from my mother.

'And the farm?'

'Oh, it was given to a relative to settle a debt.'

'Your debt?' I asked my mother.

'No.'

Like most widows of that time, Kitakkammachi owned three coarse white cotton sarees. Not even blouses to go with them, or underskirts, or underwear . . . just the sarees. What she held on to, though, was her fierce spirit and her seemingly endless love for us little ones. With all of us being home and with relatives dropping in to check on Ammachi and surreptitiously to check us out, unmarried girls, it was a summer when eligible boys and horoscopes were constantly discussed.

It was also a summer when I fancied myself in love. I was 16 years old. 'If we fall in love, what of all this jaathakam (horoscope) then?' I asked Kitakammachi.

'Do whatever you want,' she would say, 'just make sure your horoscopes match.'

When, like all good convent-educated girls, we scoffed at the idea of stars having an influence on our lives, she shushed us. 'Do you know the story of your Pedhamma?' she asked, referring to Amma's older sister, my adoptive mother. 'Pedhamma's husband's horoscope said he should only marry a girl from a family with no men; nobody paid attention to it. You know what happened?'

We fell silent. We all knew how my mama (my mother's brother) suddenly fell ill and died within a month of that wedding. We knew of my grandfather's tragic too-early death, and how my other mama had disappeared, leaving my mother's family with no men in the house.

'And do you know my story?' She continued. 'I had a dosham, which in itself would not have been a bad thing if only I had been married to a man who had more of the dosham than I did.'

We all knew how she was married at 12, to a wonderful man, who died when she was 15, leaving her with a little baby girl, my grandmother.

'What happened then,' I asked my mother that night.

'She came back home,' Amma said, 'with nothing.'

'Then how did your mother and Thatha (grandfather) get married?'

When Kitakammachi returned to her father's home, she lived under his control, obeying his every wish, until it came to her only child's marriage. Kitakammachi's daughter was to be married to her brother, a soft-spoken, kind and gentle man. Nothing wrong or unusual in that, except that Kitakammachi had spent three years with a man who had had a British education and wanted the same thing for her own daughter. She said, 'No.' She would not consider the match.

'There is a nephew, a good boy, keen on doing law, how about him?' she suggested.

When her father refused to listen, she threatened to jump into a well, along with her daughter.

The old man, not used to being defied by anyone, let alone his favourite child who was not only uneducated but also a teenage widow completely dependent on him for everything, flew into a rage and threw her out of the house. When the nephew she wanted her daughter to get married to saw her sitting on the steps outside the cattle shed, daughter in her lap, crying, and heard her story, he took her and the little child home, and when that child, Janaki, came of age at 10, he married her.

Kitakammachi lived in their home and travelled with them to Kerala, looking after her grand-babies, so her daughter could go to school, and her son-in-law could pursue his study of law. 'So if they have been through all this together, why do mother and daughter not get along,' I asked.

'Because Kitakkammachi is bold,' Amma said, 'and my mother timid, and they have no patience with each other's differences.'

I remembered her once snatching me out of the path of a scorpion and dropping a rice measure over it. We listened to the scorpion click inside its brass prison all night until the farm workers took it away the next morning.

'It could have killed you,' she admonished me. 'This is not your town with its bungalows and neat gardens, be careful.'

My mother, in an unguarded moment, confessed how once, at that very dining table where we sat, a tutor touched her inappropriately, in such a casual manner that she didn't even know whether it was deliberate or an accident, or if she had imagined it; she just knew it made her uncomfortable. She told Kitakkammachi about it and the man never came back. I heard there were not-so-quiet threats to cut his manhood off if he ever showed his face around these parts again. I couldn't get that conversation out of my head. That night it was my turn to check on Kitakkammachi. I asked her if she needed a bedpan, placed a glass of water on the night table, switched off the lights and went into the courtyard where we cousins slept on colourful jamalakams (South Indian striped flat weave rug) spread out on the floor.

'Did you hear what Amma said?' I whispered to a cousin. 'How amazing is that! To be there for each other, even if it seems like no one else would believe us, or be there for us.'

By day twelve, everyone had lost patience with Kitakkammachi's stubbornness. 'You are not going to die now,' they said, 'and we are not going to sit around either, waiting for you to leave; we have homes to go back to, and work to do.'

'Amma,' my mother reasoned gently, holding out a steel tumbler of tender coconut water, 'why are you doing this? You who never trouble anyone. You know my husband and my family are waiting for me, hundreds of miles away. I have crops in the field to tend to, and there's so much to do before the children go back to boarding school.'

Kitakkammachi looked into Amma's eyes for many minutes, then she smiled and took a sip. In a day or two, she was eating and drinking, and was back to scolding the doctor for looking at her sapotas, even going so far as to tie the dog under the sapota trees.

We children were in boarding school, and the crops had been tended to when Kitakammachi slipped in the bathroom again. The village doctor held her hands as she finally gave him the long-awaited permission to pick the precious sapotas hanging low from the trees in the front yard.

'Leave some for the children,' were her last words. 'They will be here soon to see me off.'

Kopal's Takeaway

In this book, Mahitha's story is my ode to our nanis and dadis – women who introduced us to storytelling; the ones who told us about our first heroes and villains. But after hearing Kitakammachi's story, one question lingers in my mind: Are we, as a generation, losing the courage they so effortlessly embodied?

A grandmother who stood tall and unwavering when her granddaughter was touched inappropriately by her tutor, Kitakammachi didn't hesitate, didn't falter. Her sheer courage to confront and defend is a powerful reminder of the strength and fearlessness these women carried in their hearts.

Story 12

———•———

How One Promise Took Me to the Families of 1,000 Soldiers

VIKAS MANHAS

Vikas with a fallen soldier's mother

The year was 1994. The place was Bhaderwah, in Jammu and Kashmir.

This is not the Jammu and Kashmir of Yash Chopra's romantic extravaganzas – of tulip fields and shikaras on a calm Dal Lake. This is Jammu and Kashmir where the report of a military or terrorist gun is part of your daily reality. Where each day is fraught with danger and one single misstep can mean sudden and certain death. What's more, it never lurks far, not even in the deceptively beautiful town of Bhaderwah, which is considered to be one of the most scenic parts of Jammu.

Though we were aware of the terror that could hide even in broad daylight, the sounds of gunshots that night, as we sat eating our dinner, surprised and scared us, turning the food in our mouths into ash. As the night got darker, the continuing sound of those bullets echoed even louder in our beautiful valley. Having abandoned my dinner, I was now forced to give up on sleep too – with a battle raging so close by, how could anyone sleep anyway? I turned and twisted in bed all night.

The next morning was thick with the silence that seemed to echo around the hills after the guns fell silent. But with the silence came the news – of the death of seven jawans the previous night. In an army picket where eight jawans had been deployed, seven were killed; the last man standing fought alone against the terrorists all night. Yes, alone. The seven shahid jawans were cremated in Bhaderwah itself, the town they had died defending. During that time, it was not customary to take the mortal remains of soldiers to their respective families; all that went back of the sons, fathers, brothers and husbands was their ashes, wrapped in a cloth. That was how their families said their last farewells to them.

The news of the jawans' deaths had spread far – everyone knew or had heard first-hand what transpired that night. So, the turnout at the cremation grounds was large. Bhaderwah's grateful citizens had come to pay their last respects to these seven brave men. Like everyone else, I too went for the cremation. I still remember looking at those bodies and feeling something in my gut, something I can't put down in words.

As a mere seventeen-year-old at that time, I was both young and passionate. What's more, I knew it was an important, albeit tragic, occasion for the families of the soldiers. They ought to have been here to pay their last respects. Instead, the martyrs were being bid adieu by complete strangers. Unable to wrap my head around this situation, I expressed my concerns to an army officer standing nearby. 'If we can't send the bodies of these jawans to their families, why can't we bring their families here?' I still recall his reply. He looked at me and said, 'Jo tum sochte ho, kash Dilli mein yeh koi soche.' (I wish someone in Delhi also thought like you.)

Tears streamed down my face as I stood there, feeling helpless and overwhelmed, inconsolable even by the soldier who stood holding me in his arms. I gazed into his eyes, which I noticed were also brimming with unshed tears. That day I understood that crying was a privilege only for some.

Several years passed. Had I been a painter, I would have made an attempt to capture the pain and sorrow in those eyes exactly as they had been that day. I believe that day changed me significantly; it developed in me a deep sense of empathy for our brave men in uniform and their families. When I left the cremation ground I made a promise to myself that one day I would visit the families of these soldiers.

After completing my studies, I decided to fulfil my resolve by meeting the families of those men. I thought I would visit them and share what had happened on that fateful day. I believed it would not be difficult to gather information about the soldiers and their families, since there had been numerous news articles that were written about the incident and these men. But despite my best efforts, I had no leads. Such incidents were all too common, and the news articles were routine. Every time I read an article that narrated the incidents of that night, I was transported back to that moment.

In 1999, the Kargil war erupted, and many more soldiers lost their lives. Prime Minister Vajpayee announced that the mortal remains of every soldier would be sent home, with details about their actions and bravery appearing in various newspapers. When I heard about Grenadier Uday Maan Singh, who had perished in the Kargil war, I resolved to meet his family. They were the first family I visited. I conversed with them, listening to their stories. Initially, I sat in silence, unsure of what to say. However, as the moments passed, I developed a comfort with his family. His mother pointed to a photograph and said, 'This was clicked when he came home last time – he looks so handsome resting on my lap.' It was the moment that we connected. The ice broke. She continued to speak and tell her story for the next hour but as soon as I was about to leave she asked me, 'Beta, when will you come next?'

The 'beta' in her voice felt like she was addressing her son. The thought broke my heart. As I walked out of the door, she just smiled and said, 'Phir aana, beta.' (Come again, my child.) This marked the beginning of my visits to the families of soldiers. The journey began in my mind in 1994, and after five years, I finally embarked on it. My initial hesitation was caused by the thought that my visits would reopen closed wounds. However, the bonds I formed with these families were extraordinary. They treated me like their own son. Each family I visited became a part of my own family.

To this day, I've visited over 1,000 families, and each one of them has shared countless beautiful stories with me and each of them deserves to be heard. Their emotions and experiences come alive as I recount these stories to others. People ask me about my favourite stories, a difficult choice as each story brims with love, passion and pain. Every story is inspiring. I'm still in contact with Uday Maan Singh ji's family, the first family I visited.

I often get asked, why do I spend my days doing this? Well, if the soldiers can sacrifice their lives for us, can't I dedicate my time to bringing their stories to the masses, to meet their families and spend time with them? According to my estimates, around 100,000 soldiers have lost their lives since 1947, and I aspire to recount each of their stories. Every soldier deserves the opportunity to share their experiences and if that's not possible, I want to do it on their behalf. After all, soldiers never truly die; they merely fade away. I don't need any external motivation for this. When I visit the parents of these soldiers, we exchange countless anecdotes. They offer me homemade food, and together we shed tears and share laughs. This has become a way of life for me. I will continue to visit these families throughout my life. I am now as much a part of their lives, as they are of mine.

Kopal's Takeaway

Not all privileges can be seen, and not everything we should be thankful for makes its way into our gratitude journals. Some blessings are quiet, hidden in plain sight, shaping our lives in ways we barely notice – until we stop to reflect. This story can act as a reminder for us to pause and reflect.

Story 13

He Texted Me His Last Words – But I'll Never Get a Reply

SYLVINA JENNIFER

Imagine waiting for a reply to a text you know will never come. I couldn't stop thinking about it. My thoughts were racing so fast, it was beyond anything I could imagine.

When I was 10, I met a boy at a wedding in Trichy. He, my brother and I hit it off right away, becoming fast friends. That summer became a whirlwind of firsts for me – my first bike ride, my first swim, my first Hollywood movie. The days felt like magic, and I remember it all like it was yesterday. I never wanted it to end. But as summers do, it faded, and slowly we all drifted apart and lost touch.

Fast forward to 2011. I found out he had moved to Bangalore – the same city I was living in. Excited, I looked him up on Facebook to see how life had shaped him over the years. From growing out his hair to joining a super biking club, the boy I once knew had transformed into someone entirely different.

All those old feelings came rushing back, stronger than ever. I'd always had a secret crush on him, but this time it felt like something more. As the months went by, I heard that his family was starting to look for a potential match for him. When they approached my parents, I said no. Deep down, I didn't want an arranged path – I dreamt of us falling in love naturally; having the kind of story that led to a dream wedding – not one that was decided for us.

Later that year, he got engaged, and I accepted the fact that he was never going to be mine. Although I wasn't thrilled about it, I had to come to terms with it. However, life took an unexpected turn for him, and his engagement broke. I know it sounds selfish, but I was overjoyed. A year later, he sent me a friend request on Facebook. I played it cool and accepted the request. From there, it was the usual cycle of stalking each other's profiles, liking posts and commenting on them, which eventually led to us exchanging numbers. And once that happened, there was no turning back.

We picked up right where we had left off and began talking almost every day. It seemed like he knew I was falling for him, and he made it clear that he wasn't interested in anything beyond friendship. I sensed that he had feelings for me but was holding back.

One night, he texted me asking if I was awake. I wasn't; I had gone to bed early that night. When I saw his message around 12:30 a.m., I replied, but it didn't get delivered. You know that text I was talking about at the beginning of my story? This is it.

The next morning, as per my usual routine, I went to church, but my mind was elsewhere. I found myself constantly checking my phone, anxiously waiting for his reply, unable to focus on anything else. At that moment, my brother came running towards me, and told me something that would change the course of my life forever. 'Jenny, he was in a car accident this morning, and died on the spot.' That single sentence shattered my world in an instant. Everything around me turned blurry, and I struggled to comprehend the reality of what I had just heard. I was in shock, unable to cry, as if my emotions had been frozen by the weight of the news.

On the way to the hospital, sitting in the back seat of the car, I clung to a sliver of hope that he might still be alive, that maybe it was someone else, or perhaps it was all some cruel joke. I couldn't accept the thought of him being gone.

When we arrived and I saw him lying there lifeless; the sounds of loud cries and shrieks filled the air, but I felt numb. This is when his father approached me, tears streaming down his face, and told me, 'Last night, he was talking about marrying you.' As he spoke, he burst into tears. He shared that he had left the house that morning to discuss this with a friend. All I could manage was a single tear rolling down my cheeks.

What haunts me the most is knowing that he texted me that night asking if I was awake because he wanted to tell me he wanted to marry me, but I will never be able to have that conversation with him now. I will never receive a reply to my text. My happily-ever-after ended before it even began.

I experienced the greatest heartbreak of my life. But today I share this story with you to tell you that despite enduring the most unimaginable pain, I eventually found hope. I am now happily married to a man who loves me deeply, and whom I love unconditionally. Remember, when a storm hits, pick yourself up where it left you and rebuild yourself stronger and better.

Kopal's Takeaway

I vividly remember Sylvina narrating this story in front of a live audience at one of our shows in Bangalore. She stood there, strong and courageous, while the audience wept through her words, feeling every bit of her pain. And then she delivered the final line – about finding her way out of the most devastating heartbreak and rediscovering love and happiness. The room erupted. People hooted, clapped and cheered at her resilience. That's the essence of this story: no matter how dark it gets, there is always light. Always.

Story 14

I Have a Prosthetic Leg – But I Decided to Become a Dancer

SUSHMITA CHAKRABORTY

When I was born, there were no celebrations in my family. None. In fact, my family did not want me and couldn't wait to get rid of me. Not only was I a girl, but I was a girl born with a disability – my right leg was underdeveloped, a little shorter than my left leg. The bones in my right leg hadn't fully matured and the doctor told my parents, 'She should never put pressure on her right leg, as the bones are thin and fragile.' In short, I would never be able to walk like a normal person. I had been labelled disabled at birth.

Upon discovering my condition, my family refused to have anything to do with me. They disowned me immediately after my birth, fearing it would tarnish their reputation and the respect they had built over the years in their small town of Siliguri.

Since this was still the early 1990s and not everyone had a telephone connection, my mother wrote a letter to my Nani urging her to take me away. At a time when I needed my mother's love and care the most, she abandoned me. I wonder sometimes how my life would have turned out if she had only had the courage to raise their 'disabled' daughter and raised her with love.

My Nani worked at a hospital in Kolkata; she was a busy woman with a lot of responsibilities and had her own health challenges. This made it difficult for her to take care of a newborn and she responded to my mother's letter with one of her own in which she told my parents what every parent should instinctively know – that a newborn needs her family the most and that my parents must accept me for who I was and embrace the challenges and the love I would bring to the family. However, my parents did not take Nani's advice well, and when she insisted that they keep me, they threatened to either harm me or abandon me at an orphanage. At this point, my grandmother stepped in and said she would be my guardian and has taken care of me ever since.

It was on this note that my life's journey began. Before I could even understand the world I was born into, I had already been abandoned by it. My story isn't that of abandonment though, neither is it about hate or finger-pointing. My story is one of strength, unconditional love, and resilience.

As time passed, I started realizing that my life would never be normal, not because I had a disability or because I wasn't normal, but because the people around me reduced me to my disability. When they saw me, they only saw the part of me that was missing. Those 7.5 inches of my leg. They didn't see the rest of me, the human that did exist, waiting to be acknowledged.

At school, I was treated differently. My classmates did not want to be friends with me. I was always 'that girl' for them. And so, I grew up a lonely kid, with no friends and little love. But then, something magical happened. I discovered dance. In a dance reality TV show. I would spend hours in front of the TV screen watching people dance, sway their bodies, move to the beat of the music. In those moments, I felt alive. I felt powerful. Because I had dance, I began to feel less lonely. I didn't feel the need for friends. All I wanted to do was dance. It was the only dream I had ever dreamt. I would stand before the TV and try to replicate every action I saw on screen, but of course, I wasn't even close.

At this point, I'm going to use a very cliché phrase, not because it is all I can think of, but because it has been so true for me. Yes, indeed, if there is a will, you will find a way. It is what I have come to believe, but in doing so, I have also come to strongly believe that 'if your will is extremely strong, sometimes the way will find you.'

As it did for me in 2002, the year I received my prosthetic leg at the Mahavir Seva Sadan in Kolkata.

It was not like having an actual leg of flesh and blood, but it was the closest I would get to having a 'normal' leg. The best part? It made up the 7.5 inches that were in the way of me and my passion. Despite the initial discomfort I felt, I had never felt this confident and whole before. I could now not only stand but also dance. This newfound confidence led me to participate in cultural events at my school. I began performing at school functions, despite the sympathetic looks of other people. What I needed wasn't pity but support. I recall my dance teacher modifying our performance to accommodate my need to sit, thinking I couldn't dance on my feet. Despite facing discouragement, I persisted, practised, and gradually began to find my feet and my rhythm.

Today, I dance for a living. People often ask me why I chose dancing over other pursuits.

There are many options in the world, so why dance? I guess it has something to do with what the doctor had said about me never being able to use my leg – I wanted to use my legs to dance away all my fears and sorrows, and embrace only love for my body and myself. My grandmother wished for me to have a stable career, a job in the government sector so that I could be independent and show my parents what a mistake they had made by abandoning a daughter who could have done so much to make them proud. But I didn't want my life to be about them. I didn't want to live a life where my goal was to make them regret their decision. I wanted to follow my own heart. Be my own person. Once I started performing on stage, there was no turning back. I've performed in various cities, met some beautiful people because of this art, felt alive as the audience clapped for me and cheered me on.

I believe disability isn't confined to specific organs; it's a state of mind. The day you choose to fight it, you'll feel truly liberated and as 'normal' as any human can ever feel. Society consistently aimed to make me feel inadequate due to my disability, a shortcoming I was born with, almost as though it were a sin. Indeed, disability is often treated as a sin in our country; a disabled person is deemed incapable, abnormal. Less than others. However, among the thousands of people who thought me incomplete, I also found someone who accepted me just as I am – my boyfriend. Initially, I thought my disability would prevent him from talking to me, but he proved me wrong. He makes me feel loved, he makes me feel like I deserve to be loved for who I am. With time, I also found friends who encouraged me and pushed me to make and share videos of my dances on social media – that was the start of my YouTube and Instagram pages. It was something I was very sceptical about, but on seeing the love that poured in online, there was no looking back. Today, over 100,000 people follow me on YouTube and Instagram to see me dance. There are people who will still drop mean comments on my reels but I choose to see the love. I want to live my life positively. Happily.

My parents sometimes visit my grandmother in Kolkata, but I don't meet them. However, I harbour no grudges; it is just that my entire energy is channelled towards my passion. Over twenty years of dancing, so much has changed around me. A girl who was abandoned by her family on the day she was born has found a family of millions who love her for who she is. Life is so unpredictable and so full of surprises. Next time you see a disabled person, remember my story, and don't look at them as someone different from you, look at them like you would look at someone who is choosing to be normal in a world that sees them as abnormal every single day.

Kopal's Takeaway

I discovered Sushmita's story through an Instagram reel of her dancing – and in that moment, I was in awe. Watching her move so gracefully with just one leg was more than inspiring. If your imperfections ever weigh you down, let Sushmita's journey remind you that the parts of you that feel unworthy of love are the ones that need it the most. Loving what's easy is simple; the real challenge – and beauty – lies in embracing what you or others believe doesn't deserve it.

Story 15

The Eid Journey That Reconnected Me With Humanity

NAUSHEEN KHAN

It was 'Alvida Jumma', the last Friday of Ramadan (farewell Friday of the holy month), and the emotions were palpable in the air. Right before Eid, Alvida Jumma is celebrated as the most joyful day, and like everyone, I was excited about it. Despite being away from home, I was fasting and couldn't wait to be surrounded by my loved ones. The excitement of getting back home to my mother's savoury sevaiyaan, receiving the cherished 'Eidi' – the gifts – from my grandparents, new clothes, jewellery, almost made me miss my train.

As I ran to the station to catch my train, my mother called to check in. I could barely catch my breath and told her that I would get on the train and call her back. My mother refused to cut the call and, as was quite typical of her nature, gave me a long lecture on waking up on time to avoid such situations. As I ran with my suitcase in one hand, and earphones plugged into my mother's angry voice, I suddenly sensed her tone change. She started asking me to be careful on the train, citing recent incidents involving young individuals dying due to violence and lynchings. She said, 'Beta, nowadays accidents are becoming more frequent. Recently, a 14-year-old boy was thrown out of a running car. They thought he might be carrying beef because of the way he was dressed.'

She told me to avoid carrying non-vegetarian food on the train. In a carefree tone, I responded, 'Forget non-veg, I don't even have food or water to break my fast.' Hearing this, she became even more furious and gave me another lecture.

At this point, I was only half-listening to my mother. I was rushing to catch the train and had almost lost hope, but there was the

Jhelum Express, seemingly waiting for me and the others so we could celebrate Eid with our families. I quickly rushed inside, found my seat, told my mother I was on the train, ended the call and took a deep breath.

In front of me I saw a woman who looked just like my grandmother, knitting a sweater. She seemed Punjabi, and when she saw me out of breath, she offered me water. I politely told her that I was fasting and going home for Eid. She responded, 'May God bless you more today,' which made me smile. The old lady was travelling with her husband. They introduced themselves as Gujral Uncle and Aunty. They started narrating anecdotes from their lives, one after the other. I was so engrossed in their stories that I lost track of time and didn't even realize it was iftar already. Iftar is the time when we break our fast (roza) and pray, seeking blessings from Allah. I closed my eyes, prayed and as soon as I opened my eyes I saw Uncle and Aunty had laid out food for me and said, 'Let us serve you, beta!'

I was in awe. They really didn't need to do this. It made me emotional. We enjoyed the meal together as Gujral Uncle and Aunty continued to share their stories.

The next morning, it was time for sehri – the time before dawn when we eat something because we fast for the next 12–13 hours. I was busy preparing the same for myself when Aunty woke up and saw me and said, 'Eat well, dear, you have to stay hungry the whole day.' The way she was constantly looking out for me made our little bond stronger. As the train journey was coming to an end, I was accompanied down the train by Uncle. He made sure my luggage and I were safe and sound.

As I stood at the station, the train left with Gujral Uncle and Aunty waving goodbye to me through the window. A thousand thoughts cluttered my mind. I live in a hostel and share a room with someone who performs her Hindu rituals (puja) while I read Namaz under the same roof. Yet, my mother's and society's words echo in my mind – stories of Muslim men being randomly killed or Hindus being targeted for marrying Muslims. Their concern for me is not unfounded, but it makes me feel disconnected from my own country.

I can easily say this: like me, there are many others who feel safe and hopeful as long as Jalandhar has a Gujral Uncle, Gujarat has a Mehta Uncle, Madhya Pradesh has a Khan Uncle, Mumbai has a D'Souza Aunty, and Chennai has a Pillai Uncle. As long as these people exist we are safe, we are one, we are united. Today I can say that I woke up to hope, and I will continue to find this hope everywhere I go.

Kopal's Takeaway

My takeaway is simple: I want to share as many stories as possible that remind us of the goodness in people. Stories like Nausheen's have the power to dissolve hate, inspire love and remind us that kindness can prevail even in the toughest times. No matter who you are or where you come from, I hope you encounter stories that rekindle your faith in humanity. These stories remind us that love should always triumph over hate and that despite our differences, we are meant to coexist and uplift one another.

Story 16

Why the 'Perfect Wedding' Isn't as Perfect as We Think

SHRUTI SONAL

In the month of March, when Delhi was yet to turn into a boiler room, I went to watch the film *Laapata Ladies* in the theatre. I was alone. In my nearly three decades of existence, it's one of the joys I've hung on to: watching films by myself in dark theatres, having no one to share my popcorn with or ask questions. It's just me and the film.

Yet, as I watched this slice of life film about two brides who go missing during a train journey, leading to a chaotic search, I did not feel alone. I felt like I was surrounded by so many women from my family, many of whom had been in situations eerily similar to the characters. Sure, maybe they hadn't ended up getting physically lost after their weddings, but there were other kinds of losses. Other kinds of purdahs. As I watched the credits roll, the stories came rushing back. Stories from a place far from the national capital, where I come from, but always struggled to belong.

Begusarai, that's where my parents live. It's a small district in the state of Bihar, which has seen its fair share of floods and riots over the years. In politics, it is one of the few pockets in the state (and the country) where the Left dominated for years, leading to it being called the 'Leningrad of Bihar'. Yet, it's infamous in pop culture for its crimes. There was even a TV show that ran back in 2015 by the name of *Begusarai*, which didn't help with the stereotypes. Home to over 2,00,000 people, it is also known for something else: pakadua vivah. As most young men left the place in search of better prospects, the few remaining eligible grooms would be kidnapped (sometimes at gunpoint) and made to sit on mandaps by families struggling to find a match for their daughters. The fear was real. On many occasions, my father recalls how boys in his college would always walk together in groups to avoid being picked up in this manner. That, of course, reminded me of how girls in my college did that too, in Delhi's lanes.

Things have become slightly better over the years, although news about such kidnapping instances still makes it to local newspapers. However, while things may have improved for men, marriage continues to be a sombre affair for most women. My aunt, who got married sometime in the 1980s, found *Laapataa Ladies* too close to home. Not only was the ghoonghat that she wore equally long but so was the feeling of being lost. 'We were hardly told anything. I didn't even know my to-be husband's address. I was just put on a train, along with him and my brother,' she said to me.

Although my mother did not ever speak to me candidly about her own marriage, I often wonder what would have become of her if she had had the freedom to pursue her dreams. She preferred books to preparing meals in the kitchen. The drive was so much that despite a lack of resources, she came top of her class, and was one of the few women from Begusarai to pursue a PhD at that time. However, being the eldest daughter in a family of six siblings, she was married off before she finished college. After that, she never worked. Something or the other always came in her way: kids, health, patriarchy. After her death, I have spent a long time thinking about how different her life could have been. I've gone through albums and albums of photographs, yet what strikes me the most is her wedding photo: she has no smile on her face, as she gazes directly into the camera.

In the narrow lanes of Begusarai, most young women, even today, do not have a partner who says, 'I love you' to them and blushes. There, the picture-perfect and Instagrammable photographs of Bollywood couples laughing candidly at their weddings seem like a distant dream. In fact, smiling is often scorned, I learnt some years ago.

It was 2011. I had gone to my village to attend my cousin's wedding. Hours before the muhurat, chaos ensued. The groom's side, at the last moment, increased their demand for dowry. A two-wheeler wouldn't do, they wanted a car instead. Nothing less than a Honda. If this wish wasn't fulfilled, they threatened to not show up. Everyone scrambled, put together the money for the down payment, and bought a car on EMI. Several lakhs worth of cash and gold had already been given to the groom's family.

On the day of the wedding, there was hardly any sign of laughter. Yet, there was some relief too. My cousin had crossed the age of thirty and had what some call a 'wheatish' complexion. If more time went by, the prospective grooms would have only asked for more dowry. At least it was done and dusted. As she put on her bright red lehenga, her friends joked about the length of her ghoonghat. Meanwhile, the makeup artist put on a shade of foundation that was at least five shades lighter than my cousin's skin colour. Dabs of Fair and Lovely cream were also applied, in a last-ditch attempt to forge a different reality.

The baraat came three hours behind schedule, and the groom's friends continued dancing for another two, even as drops of sweat mixed with the bride's makeup. For the next few hours, the mantras dragged on. With the exception of a few fleeting moments, my cousin sobbed throughout. I was taken aback: was this a wedding or a funeral? Behind me, many aunties chit-chatted. 'Look at her, crying so much. How sweet of her!' one of them said.

That day, I learnt that tears were a prerequisite for being called a sanskari bride. Nearly seven years later, my cousin's younger sister got married in a similar fashion. In fact, she cried so much that in all her photographs her face seemed swollen. At one point, she nearly fainted from exhaustion in the brutal May heat. The aunties approved. I was appalled, and at some point, struck up a conversation with my uncle about how depressing this was. In response, he asked me if I was a communist. I laughed in response.

Yet, in my phase of naivety, I thought such things only happened in Begusarai. Surely, things would change for the women who made it out of the town. The world would be at our feet. We could study and earn and dream. We could smile at our weddings too. I was in for a rude shock.

If you search on Google you'll know that the distance between Begusarai and Delhi is over a thousand kilometres. Yet, it felt like two completely different worlds. For the longest time I believed that teary-eyed brides, burgeoning demands of dowry and caste fissures were something that people left behind when they came to the national capital. Over the years, cinema too made me believe that a wedding is the best day of a girl's life. In the movies, the brides were always happy, smiling and dancing like the groom. They'd shed a tear when hugging their mothers, but only fleetingly. I was told that if we worked hard enough we could have the best of both worlds: professional and personal. Unlike our mothers and aunts and older siblings, we didn't have to sacrifice our dreams at the altar of marriage. In some ways, it was true. Every time I found myself taking a solo trip or watching a film by myself in a dark theatre, a part of me always whispered: you might be the first woman in your family to be doing this. It was liberating, yet it also put a certain sense of responsibility on my shoulders. I better make some use of it, I told myself. In my mother's absence, the feeling only magnified. I had to live all the lives she never got to, I repeated to myself.

Slowly, I also began to forge deeper bonds with women my age and started seeing weddings in a softer light. Even as I grappled with questions of the life I wanted for myself, I had fun at shaadis. A few months ago, in Jharkhand's

Jamshedpur, my cousin brother's bride entered the wedding stage dancing to the beats of the dhol. She sang along to the Bollywood songs that played. She laughed her heart out. Many were offended. I cheered on. 'See, things are changing,' a part of me said.

Yet, as if to break my bubble, another experience followed. A cousin sister, younger to me in age, called me crying one day. She is one of the brightest in our family, and did everything that a woman of her potential is told to: she cracked the NEET, got enrolled in a medical college in Delhi and gave her best. Back in the village, her name was taken with pride. However, as years passed and she reached her 'shaadi' age, the bitter realities came to light. After a long-term relationship ended on a bad note, her parents started pushing her to see other rishtas. As things unfolded it came to light that not much has changed. Even the families of fellow male doctors wanted hefty dowries. Her overweight physique became the topic of ridicule in many conversations. And her professional ambitions were often seen in a negative light. The process started taking a toll on her mental and physical health so much that she found it difficult to get out of bed. Sometimes, she fought back against the system that belittled all that she had achieved. At other times, she was too tired to do that. In moments of exasperation, her parents often questioned if they had given her 'too much freedom', which had made her rebellious (and unmarriageable).

Too much freedom. It's a term I've heard many times in my life, but it breaks my heart every single time. Yes, I am aware. Women are joining the army and flying planes. They are topping university exams and leading multi-billion dollar companies. Yet, it's possible for many realities to coexist, not just in our villages, but also in our cities.

In reality, finding a happy ending for women is typically a lot more complicated than in a film. In the fictional village of 'Nirmal Pradesh' in *Laapata Ladies*, for instance, caste barriers hardly exist. Men are soft and ready to call out their friends in sexist situations. Women of all ages have a desire to change their fates. And perhaps most importantly, police personnel play their roles constructively.

In real life, the absence of even one of these elements often proves to be a full stop to the dreams of many young women. The only thing we can do, perhaps, is stand up for them when the time comes: by lending an ear, opening our arms and seeing them for who they are. Seeing our mothers for who they are. Seeing our own selves for who we are. Not superhumans but the product of a struggle that continues. Let's dance, sing and smile to that.

Kopal's Takeaway

Girls, things haven't changed enough, have they? If your parents are pressuring you into a marriage, do you know what you'll do? Will you say 'yes' just to keep them happy? That's okay – I might, too.

But before you decide, take a moment to think about this: What do you truly want? Do you see yourself happy in this decision a year or ten from now? Marriage should be about partnership, not pressure. If it doesn't feel right, it's okay to pause, reflect and speak up.

Remember, saying 'yes' out of obligation isn't your only option. Your happiness and choices matter just as much as anyone else's.

Story 17

I Wanted to Be Tendulkar, But That One Day Changed My Life

KRISHNA IYER

After two years, I stepped on to the cricket ground. In spite of the passage of time, I walked on to the crease like it was just another day, ready to play, filled with childlike excitement.

They say in India every gully has a Tendulkar, and I had always been that boy in my gully. The boy who lived, breathed, ate, dreamt cricket. On all days and at all times. The extent of my obsession painted the walls of my house red with rubber-ball patches.

However, in the two years, a lot had changed in my life but everything on the field had remained the same: Nishant was still the wicketkeeper, Salil continued to be the pro-batsman who always opened with me and, when it came to fielding, Ashwin and I would be near the boundary. We lost the toss, and as a result, we were going to be fielding first. I was looking forward to some great action on the field. As always, I stood near the boundary because I had a powerful throw and the best judgement for long-distance catches. I was positioned at deep mid-wicket.

The first time the ball came towards me, I ran forward to pick it up. As I approached it, the ball passed me on my left. I had completely misjudged the ball's position. Without thinking much about it, I continued to play. But then it happened multiple times – I was continuously misjudging the trajectory of the ball, missing catches and getting knocked on the head a couple of times.

However, I wasn't going to let one innings deter my spirits. I excused myself under the pretext of poor practice and told myself that these things were bound to happen since I was playing after a couple of years. I consoled myself with the thought that I would be opening our innings when it came time to bat, and that things would be fine once I got cracking then.

So the second innings began. Salil and I opened the game.

At the first delivery, I couldn't judge the speed of the ball. What happened while fielding seemed to repeat itself. I stood stunned, unable to fathom my own misjudgement of the ball's movement. I asked my friend to bowl again and somehow, with shaky hands and shivering eyelids, I managed to make contact with the ball. The reality was that my eyes couldn't adjust to the speed of the ball.

For short-pitch deliveries and good-length balls, I went on the back foot to play them. That had never been my style, I used to enjoy batting and dancing down the pitch. Usually, when a player is unable to face fast-paced deliveries, they try a shot with the spin balls. So I asked my friend to bowl a spinner. I had no sight of the ball after the first bounce. The shift caused by the spin after that bounce seemed unfathomable to my eyes.

A hundred thoughts ran through my head. Maybe it has been a while, maybe the sun is scorching hot, maybe I wasn't paying attention? *But when did I ever have to pay attention?* I thought to myself. My game was spot on, irrespective of practice or attention.

A small voice in my head told me that it was over, but another told me that I couldn't give up.

So the next time, in an exasperated tone, I told him to deliver a slower ball, and I just about managed to place the ball on the off side. By then, I knew it was over. The eyes that could once spot the cricket ball in a pitch-dark ground couldn't read a simple spin delivery. The eyes that never missed a catch now seemed afraid of an approaching ball.

I still remember how delighted I had been when Dad bought me my first bat. It was a Kashmir willow with a fine stroke.

But today, the bat in my hand was just a

piece of wood. It had lost its purpose. I was the magician who couldn't get the magic right any more. I felt like a kid who had lost his parents in a crowded fair. The feeling of loss sank in slowly, the feeling of home became a distant memory, and I felt a pit growing in my belly that I could not climb out of.

I was short of words to express what I felt. How do I explain how easy it had been to play any delivery effortlessly? How do I convince myself that I could not play like that any more? That those twenty-two yards would never be the same for me?

Time and again people told me that a good amount of practice would bring me back to form and I would play like before. But I could never explain to them how good a cricketer I had been at one point in time. It almost felt like asking, 'Can you unlearn how to walk? Can you unlearn how to cycle?'

Until that day, my accident or the disability caused by the accident never bothered me.

When I was 15 years old, I met with a car accident. An iron rod pierced my forehead and I was surviving on life support (ventilator) for forty-four days. On the forty-sixth day, I observed in the mirror that my forehead had a ripe wound with a few stitches on it. What was more surprising was that my right eyelid wouldn't open completely. There was a squint in the eye. The doctors said that the third cranial nerve had died. The third cranial nerve is responsible for eyelid functioning. For almost a year after the accident I was on bed rest, immobile. Partially, it took a toll on my memory. Recollecting incidents and events took time for me. I couldn't read for long hours. In spite of this, I managed to clear my SSC exams after studying for a month. Every day, I discovered minor disabilities, but that didn't deter my confidence. Until that day, my accident or the disability caused by the accident had never bothered me. But that day, reality hit me, and it hit hard. Because until then, I was used to hearing 'You've been a miracle child. Of all the children in the accident, you were the luckiest and recovered the soonest.'

But for me it was a feeling of being punched in my gut. I felt choked. I was unable to understand and accept that my vision had been compromised. I fell on my knees on the ground and wept like a helpless child. Shivers ran down my spine when I realized that it was over for me. I had goosebumps all over my body.

At once, I wanted to rewind time. I wished the night of the accident had never happened. I wished I had never sat in that car. I wished I hadn't gone that night. I wanted to scream out aloud, why? Why me?

I don't remember how the accident happened. I was knocked out on the spot and the next thing I knew, I was in the hospital ward. It felt like I was cheated overnight, like the forces of nature played a dirty game with me and I lost the most important power I possessed. It was no longer just an injured eye, it was the end of my cricketing dream. The truth was like an invisible knife that kept piercing deeper and deeper into me with the passage of time. I continued my life without any qualms until that day on the field.

It's been more than fifteen years since the accident and about thirteen years to this day. Life has changed almost in every aspect but every time I watch a match there's a pricking sensation in my heart. The mere realization that cricket is nothing but a childhood memory of good times is how I have made peace with grief. We realize loss in different ways perhaps. It was then that I realized what I lost. Innumerable attempts to get over it seemed to fail because nothing can replace the excitement and the adrenaline of playing a match and hitting the ball across the boundary line.

Grief prevails with the memories like two streams running parallel to each other. On the bad days, you wish for another chance and on the good ones, you reminisce about those days with a smile on your face. I wish the story of my dream was like a Bollywood movie, where despite all the hurdles, the hero gets his heroine, in my case, my dream to be a cricketer. But real life isn't a Bollywood film, and I don't have a happy ending to conclude my story but here is one thing I can say: if you are where I was thirteen years ago, life does have its own plans for you, perhaps not the one you imagined for yourself, but the one that was meant for you. Cherish what you have, for regrets don't pay for the losses.

Kopal's Takeaway

If there is a god of cricket, he's certainly Indian and he's probably Sachin Tendulkar – a young boy from Mumbai with big dreams and an even bigger determination. He made it. Every Indian knows his name, every Indian has seen him play and every Indian has cheered for him. But what about those who want to be him? His tale is one that has planted a million dreams. Every young child who plays cricket – whether in their colony park, school, building lobby or gully, breaking a windowpane here and a rear-view mirror there – wants to be him. A dreamer, when he or she makes it big, does something magical – they make others dream. This is the story of an eleven-year-old boy who batted really well and whom his gully cricket friends referred to as 'Tendulkar'. What a prize to win! But where there's a dream, there is also a fear of it shattering into pieces. What happens when dreams don't come true? What happens when life gets in the way of one's ambitions, as in the case of this other boy from Mumbai? Krishna Iyer's story is the story of most of us because not all dreams come true, and if we don't tell these stories, we will never learn to live with our losses.

Story 18

How Speaking Up Saved Me

AARTI KUBER

'Teachers live forever in hearts they touch.'

I was just thirteen when I realized that what my maths teacher was doing to me was called molestation. Even though I had no words for it until then, I was wise enough to know that there was something seriously wrong with the way he touched me. It made me shudder and cringe. It was only when I was taught the difference between good touch and bad touch that I learnt that the touch was deemed inappropriate by others too! With this realization, a whole lot of rage began to build up in my innocent heart. As I was still too young to understand it, my body stored it as aches and pains that still return to trouble me sometimes.

Everything that Google tells you about child sexual abuse and its symptoms – social anxiety, an inability to be alone with my thoughts, disconnection from my instincts and bodily sensations – was true for me. The experience was so shattering that I was unable to trust even my own family and friends. I had absolutely nothing to hold on to, both within myself and around me. These repeating patterns made me feel like I was lost in the midst of a constantly crumbling world.

Somehow, I got through school. I think I managed it because those awful memories were tucked away in my subconscious mind where I couldn't access them. But when I reached college, the memories resurfaced when I least expected it. So, my teenage self resorted to addictions to escape the painful reality. Eventually, when I hit rock bottom, I went for therapy. That's when my life began to transform. I started taking care of myself and giving my inner child the love that she needed, and everything was different.

You might have heard that your vibe attracts your tribe. In my last year of college, I began attending and co-facilitating support group circles for survivors of abuse. It was here that I made friends who understood me. The solidarity and hope I found from sharing my story and listening to others empowered me to take a courageous step.

During a writing exercise in one of our sessions, I wrote a letter to my maths teacher. Over time, I felt the need to confront him. A part of me was terrified to go ahead, but my friends reassured me that my need for closure was valid. They agreed to accompany me and hold me through it all.

Walking up to his doorstep and ringing his doorbell with my trusted friends by my side felt so surreal. I almost couldn't believe it was really happening, but I knew that I needed to do this for myself. Here's the letter that I read out to him and his wife that evening in December 2016:

It's been 10 years since the first time you molested me.

It's been 10 years since I chose to remain silent.

But just two years later – on 26 November 2008 to be exact – I knew that something was wrong.

I would try to come for the tuition class only when your wife was home. One day, I came at night to submit my test paper in which I got all the sums right. Unfortunately, she had gone to watch a movie and you took full advantage of that situation. It's funny you had the nerve to call my parents and ask them why I hadn't been coming to class after that.

Although we live nearby and run into each other often, I didn't say a thing. So I decided now to get up here and do it. No, I'm not scared of you, but I can see that you are scared of me. You run away every time you see me and cannot even bear to look me in the eye.

Why didn't I take any action up until now?

Because I had no intention of harming your family. I couldn't understand how you could do such a thing when you have a wonderful and intelligent daughter and a beautiful wife. That just eludes me. I chose to see the best in you. I was an innocent child. You corrupted me, destroyed me by groping me with those hands and feet. Yes, I remember how you'd caress my leg under the table with your feet. I hope you realize that you cannot undo these things you've done.

I cringe at the thought of you doing this to other children. I often confront you in my dreams so I decided to actually take this step to express myself.

You do not need to apologize to me because you know what? I've already forgiven you. I don't think it's my job to take any sort of revenge. Both science and religion say that what goes around comes around. And I sincerely pray that your family does not take that hit for you. Not only did you permanently scar me, but you also gave me an undying fear of mathematics.

Just so you know, I have and will continue to work with survivors of sexual abuse and empower them until they become as strong as I feel today standing in front of you. Today I am letting you go from my mind and my thoughts.

Once I was done, his wife stepped forward and gave me a hug. She told me that years ago he had confessed to her and they had both made peace for the sake of the family. She said that he had come a long way since then and regretted his actions. He was there all the while, hiding behind the door, but he didn't leave even though I know this could not have been easy for him.

Finally, he emerged from behind the door and told me he was really sorry that he didn't realize how his actions would affect me. At that moment I knew I could do two things: be bitter about what he said to me or let it go. I chose the second option and here I am today, living a life where that incident doesn't define me any more.

I don't regret anything that happened. I don't regret the pain and suffering I experienced, because, through it, I could connect with the raw and real parts of others. At a tender age, I witnessed the injustice in our world and through that, I understood the importance of loving, of being kind and forgiving. It was when I felt seen and heard by people who cared for me that I began to get better and find myself again.

Sexual violence is a topic that makes a lot of people angry, as it should. However, as a survivor of abuse, I realized being angry did nothing but burn me some more. Underneath it, I found the voice of my inner child. She wanted me to follow my heart, chase my dreams and live my life with joy and freedom. She told me that I'm not alone in this and that there are so many others with similar experiences. I realized that I am so much more than what happened to me!

I believe in the adage that goes 'Hurt people, hurt people, and healed people, heal people.' So, instead of diluting my essence, I chose to take the time and space to tend to my heartache and witness the beauty that emerged from it. I found that then I could be present for those around me as a therapist – whether personally or professionally. I hope to see our society change in the way we respond to these situations and bring more compassion so that we can move beyond surviving to thriving.

Kopal's Takeaway

According to a 2007 study by the Indian government, more than 53 per cent of children in India have experienced one or more forms of sexual abuse. Given its high prevalence, it's likely that a significant number of people reading this may have experienced situations similar to Aarti's. If you have, please remember that you are not alone and your experience is valid.

Not everyone may feel ready or have the resources to confront their abuser or embark on a healing journey right away – and that's okay. Healing is deeply personal and looks different for everyone. Whether it's speaking to someone you trust, seeking professional support or simply acknowledging your feelings, every step – no matter how small – is a testament to your courage.

> 'Hurt people, hurt people; healed people, heal people' is a phrase that has opened my eyes to so many different perspectives on pain, healing and compassion, and I hope it does the same for you. Aarti's journey has taught me that when we heal ourselves, we become a source of healing for others.

Story 19

———•———

How a Simple Auto Ride Changed My Life Forever

RITIKA SONI

From left to right: Suhani Shah, Ritika Soni, Bhola Bhaiya, Kopal Khanna

'Uncle, who is Seema?' I asked the auto driver, Bhola Uncle, about the name written on the back of his auto.

'My wife,' he replied, his eyes distant and moist.

I was heading home after college. My auto was crawling through the busy streets of Mumbai. They say Mumbai is a city of dreams, but having lived here for over two years now, I know that it is actually a city of dreamers! From attending college in the daytime to following my passion of performing storytelling and poetry in the evening, I would often find myself standing in the middle of a busy road wondering where I belonged. It was one such evening. I stood listening to the cacophony of the traffic on the city's streets, and as the beeps and horns slowly receded into the distance, muffled by the sound of the thoughts in my head, I was suddenly brought back to my immediate surroundings by the voice of a man. An auto driver. He asked me, 'Kahan jaana hai?' (Where do you want to go?) In a city like Mumbai, where you face rejections from auto drivers day in and day out, this was nothing short of a miracle. I told him I wanted to go to Dadar, and he agreed to drop me there.

After spending some time in the auto, my curiosity got the better of me, so I said, 'You know, I got rejected by ten auto drivers before you stopped.' Gazing at my reflection in his rear-view mirror, he grinned and said, 'Beta, as soon as I slide into the driver's seat, I am an auto driver, a man whose job is to take people from one place to another. Why should I say no to anyone? If a person is out on the roads, it is because he has somewhere to go. I merely try to make sure I help them reach where they are headed.'

His words, I realized, belonged to someone who had abandoned his journey midway for only that person could know the true value of a journey.

'Where do you live?' I asked him next.

'I run this auto the whole day, and sleep in a temple at night,' he replied nonchalantly as though it were the most normal thing to do in the world.

At times, we come across individuals who resemble aged books stored within a library, eagerly waiting for someone to brush off their dust and uncover the story within the covers.

'Why in a temple?' I asked him, even more curious now to know his life story.

'My mother died five days after giving birth to me. Soon after, my father remarried. At the age of ten, I ran away from brutal domestic violence and started working in a power loom in Mumbai. After a few years when I married my soulmate, I thought my life had finally begun to blossom. But things don't go your way, do they? My boss fired me and I was suddenly jobless. That's when my wife gave me all her savings and asked me to buy this auto. While I was running the auto day in and day out, Seema would care for our four boys.' This was the first time I'd heard his wife's name from his mouth. The name that was written on his auto, it made sense now.

He continued, 'Then one day my wife developed a severe stomach ache, and after a few tests, the doctor declared that she had cancer. I have never seen the sky fall, but that day I realized what it must feel like. Without wasting a single minute, I admitted her to a hospital in Mumbai. I took out a loan to bear the expenses, sold our house, and we started sleeping in a temple.' He was telling me his story as if he had been waiting for a listener for so long and had finally found one. I felt like a friend was pouring his heart out.

He then said, 'But that was not the worst of

it. The worst was learning that my loved one's life depended on the expensive medicines and treatments that I couldn't afford. From mandir to gurudwara, I prayed everywhere to save her from this monstrous cancer, because I believed that even if God couldn't appear to help me, he would send me an angel. Then one day while waiting outside the doctor's cabin, our angel appeared – in the form of a generous man. He came out of nowhere and volunteered to help us monetarily. If this is not a miracle, then I don't know what is! My wife said that it was a reward for my kindness over all these years because no kind action goes in vain. You see, with her sweet words and her beautiful smile, she could win over anyone.' He paused and smiled. I did too.

'But unfortunately, no amount of money could save her. Despite the treatment, help and prayers, we couldn't save her. And now all I have left of her is her name on my auto and a heart full of her memories.' Wiping my own tears, I asked him 'How are you doing now?'

He said, 'When someone you love dies, a part of you also dies with them. Things have started getting better now, but at night when I go back to the temple to sleep, I wish my wife was there with me. People often blame God for their miseries, but I think the energy that runs this whole world will not give you pain without reason. The only complaint I have with God is, "Kaash ek beti de diye hote" (I wish he had given us a daughter) because no one can love you like your mom, wife or daughter!'

We both sat in silence until we reached my destination because sometimes words are no longer necessary. And sharing a silence feels infinitely more powerful. I got off the auto and asked him if there was any way in which we could stay in touch. Instantly he took out his phone and asked me to take his number. When I looked up at him to ask his name, he replied, 'Bhola.' His smile at that moment was as innocent as his name.

Life went on, I took hundreds of different autos and met all sorts of people, but one particular night I found myself lost among the crowd of this city. My heart yearned for a familiar face that could calm the strange panic that was beginning to rise within me. And then suddenly, out of nowhere, I took out my phone and dialled Bhola Uncle's number. Calling him that day was as random as his agreeing to come instantly to meet me. But the most random things in life always turn into the most beautiful stories.

That day, Uncle and I sat over a cup of chai and talked about different things. He told me about his elder son who was soon going to get married and the youngest one who was waiting for his board results. The loan that he had taken for his wife's treatment was almost repaid now. I told him how I had found a job but was not getting enough time to follow my passion. Though we both belonged to two completely opposite worlds, a bridge of trust and vulnerability connected us. A few hours ago, I had felt nothing but anger for the world, for being the overwhelming place it seemed sometimes, but after meeting him, I realized people like him make this world a better place for people like me.

As I sat talking to him, I could sense my worries dissipate. 'Uncle,' I said, 'thank you so much for coming today and meeting me. I feel like I am at home but I am sorry for calling you out of the blue like this.'

I was expecting him to give me a goodbye smile, but he angrily said, 'Which daughter in this world says thank you to her father for being there for her? If you are not feeling good, it's my duty to be with you until you feel better again, that's what family is for.'

Before I could process what he had just said, he went on, 'You remember I always had just one complaint to take up with God, he didn't give me a daughter, but now I don't have that complaint also,' and gave me a pat on my head, which felt like nothing less than the warm protective hand of a father. Since that day, he has been there for me whenever I need him, and I try to put a smile on his face whenever we speak. It's truly my most special bond.

From feeling all alone in a strange city to finding a home in a stranger, life came full circle. Sometimes the family you choose becomes your home – not familiar at first but embracing you with warmth and comfort when you need it the most.

Kopal's Takeaway

I've had the privilege of meeting both Ritika and Bhola ji in Mumbai, and their bond is truly remarkable. Their connection is a beautiful reminder of how sometimes the most meaningful relationships are forged in the most unexpected ways. This story has my heart, for it celebrates the depth of human connection and the unwavering power of love, loyalty and family.

Story 20

Does Anyone Have an Extra Pen? A Story of Friendship and Loss

DUSHYANT SINGH

Who doesn't cherish a true friendship? And why not? After all, we choose our friends and for most of us they are the people we feel closest to. People we hang out with, vent to, whose advice we take each time we fall in love and whose shoulder we cry on after a break-up. Everyone needs a friend by their side.

And I had one. From the time I was in school.

His name was Bhupinder, Bhupinder Pal Singh, also known as Ronnie.

Ronnie may have been a head shorter than me, but when it came to friendship, he set the bar high. Whether it was getting together to fly kites on Makar Sankranti or taking the blame for breaking Mr Sharma's glass window, Ronnie was always ahead of everyone else.

I met him the day I joined my new school. When I walked into my classroom on the first day, the teacher made me sit next to him. No sooner had I sat down than he asked me, 'Hey! Do you have an extra pen?'

And that's how our friendship began.

I did not know it then, but this was Ronnie's go-to sentence, something he used as an icebreaker to initiate a friendship. A pick-up line so to speak, but for a friend. Over the years, I witnessed him use it with numerous others because he loved to make friends. But our bond was special.

He was the Sonu to my Titu. The Yuvraj to my Dhoni. If I were a pen and this story my ink, he would be the cap that kept me from drying out. But where there is friendship, there is also pain.

I remember the day so clearly. It was our Grade 7 final exam. Middle-class children often carry the weight of their parents' dreams. So, I took my studies and exams seriously, making sure I completed the entire syllabus and revised it ahead of the papers. Once in the examination hall, I focused on my work, avoiding eye contact and keeping my answers hidden. These were useless commands ingrained in me since childhood, but I followed them. They seem unnecessary to me now but I didn't know any better back then. That day, during the exam, Ronnie asked me a question, but I refused to cheat and give him the answer. My refusal hurt him.

After the exam, when I tried talking to him, he turned silently and walked away. He ignored my calls, disconnected the phone, didn't reply to any of my messages, and refused to interact with me during the holidays. When I thought about it, I realized I had hurt him deeply because unlike me, he wasn't thinking of this as a mere five-mark question that I hadn't helped him answer. For him my refusal signified something bigger – it signified that I had not been there for my friend when he was in trouble, it signified that I preferred to uphold my stupid principles over our friendship.

Guilt wounds never heal, but with time, you learn to live with them. I made many efforts to make him understand, to talk, to resolve the situation, but everything was in vain. Maybe it was better to let time heal that wound. So, I did just that. I started sitting with Abhi. Abhi was my friend too, but he was more sophisticated, a genius with the potential to crack into IIT, and like everyone else, I had a deep respect for him. But our relationship was not a patch on my friendship with Ronnie, whom I missed every day.

Then one day, during our English lesson, which happened to be just before recess, I felt hungry and decided to risk taking a quick bite from my lunchbox while the class was in progress. Neerja Ma'am, our English teacher, had the nose of a bloodhound and it did not take long for her to smell the aroma of my mother's food. She was not happy about it. Code red was activated.

At first, she asked us kindly: 'Whoever is eating from their lunchbox, please stand up voluntarily, it won't end well if I find out.' I felt like this offer was more like a trap. My instinct for self-preservation nudged me from within, 'This is a bait, don't fall for it. Stay seated, Dushyant.' I did what my instinct told me was the right thing to do. I remained seated. Then Neerja Ma'am asked a second time, 'Honestly, stand up if you're eating from the lunchbox, otherwise strict action will be taken.' This time, it was fear that held me back.

Frustrated by such blatant dishonesty she decided to take action. 'Now, I will inspect the lunchboxes. Gargi, you check the girls' lunchboxes, and Ronnie, you check the boys' lunchboxes.' My heart pounded with fear, which was evident on my face too as sweat dripped from my forehead. I was sure I was about to get caught. After checking the lunchboxes of three students, Ronnie asked for my lunchbox, and with trembling hands, I handed it to him.

He looked at it, closed it, and put it back inside my bag. 'Madam, Dushyant hasn't brought a lunchbox today.' And in that single moment I knew I wanted to hug Ronnie and cry.

During recess, I approached him and said, 'Ronnie, I'm sorry! Forgive me, my friend.'

He remained silent for a while, then said, 'The next period is social studies, which I find very boring. Sit next to me or else I'll tell Neerja Ma'am the truth.'

And just like that, everything was fine again. Everything was sorted, and a sense of calmness returned.

After Grade 12, I decided to pursue Engineering and Ronnie decided to try his luck with an MBBS degree. Ronnie and I may not have been sitting together in the same class, but we still found time to share all our stories over phone calls. After college, I got a job in Mysore.

Finding time for each other became difficult once the real world began to catch up with us. My work routine and assessments kept me so busy that it had been almost two months since I last spoke to Ronnie.

Then suddenly, one evening, news came that Ronnie had had an accident and was in a critical condition. My world seemed to come to a grinding halt. It felt as though someone would shake me and I would wake up to find myself back in Neerja Ma'am's class where I would tell Ronnie what a nightmare I'd had. But no, this was no nightmare. This was as real as life can get.

By the time I caught my flight and reached the hospital where he was admitted, it was already too late. Drinking and driving took his life. It has been eight years since that incident, and it has taken me a long time to learn to live with this truth.

There is one last apology I want to make, just one.

To Ronnie, if you can still hear me.

Please forgive me. Forgive me for not being there when you were fighting alone for your life, forgive me for not being able to hear your last words.

Sorry, Ronnie! If possible, please forgive me, my friend.

And I have only two things to say to all of you. These friends you have are incredibly precious, valuable and rare. Keep them safe, keep them secure, and don't let them drive when they are drunk, no matter how much they insist on it. Second, 'Does anyone happen to have an extra pen?'

> **Kopal's Takeaway**
>
> Friendships are incredibly important, yet in pop culture, they often take a back seat to love, which is seen as the ultimate bond. Dushyant's story is a poignant reminder of the deep value friendships hold in our lives. It shows us that these connections, though sometimes fleeting, shape us in profound ways. Good things don't always last forever, which is why we must cherish and nurture our bonds while we have them.

Story 21

The Day I Pretended To Be an Alcoholic

EISHA CHOPRA

My name is Eisha. And I'm an alcoholic.

This is the story of a night that changed my life. It was an early evening in late March, almost ten years ago. I had just started thinking about becoming a professional actor and a friend had recommended that I speak to one of his colleagues as it would help me gain a fresh perspective, which is much-needed in the acting journey. This was someone who had been active on the Delhi theatre scene for many years, and my friend thought it was a good way for me to get a foot in the door. I was happy to meet him, but when I got there I realized he wasn't any random person, he was someone I had heard of. He was Sukhi. Sukhi, the alcoholic.

In fact, he was one of Delhi's most famous alcoholics. I'd heard many stories about him because he was one of the few people to actually talk about his struggle with alcoholism.

One of the first things he asked me when we met was, 'Why do you want to become an actor? Why do you want to get on stage?'

I told him, it's because I like to feel things. I want to feel all the highs and the lows a human being can feel and real life doesn't give the same opportunities that stories do. He agreed.

We started speaking about other things, and the conversation just flowed.

I learnt that he was now clean. Not one sip of alcohol in eighteen years. I had a lot of questions for him. 'So, now you're no longer an alcoholic? That's great,' I said.

To which he responded, 'I'll always be an alcoholic, my dear. I just don't drink any more.

It's a disease. Like diabetes. You don't stop being diabetic, you just stop taking sugar.'

Sukhi and I became friends really fast, even though he was thirty years older. After meeting him a few times, he even started calling me 'Krishnamurti', after the great Indian philosopher, because our conversations always had a philosophical bent.

Time went by and our conversation moved from one topic to another. I was totally enamoured by Sukhi. After a little while longer, he began glancing at his watch every now and then.

'I have to go. I have my AA meeting at 7 … but you know what, Krishnamurti ? Why don't you come with me? Because I think you should attend an AA meeting to know what it feels like to be there. Besides, this is an open meeting, and everyone is invited.'

And that's how I got to my first Alcoholics Anonymous meeting. An open meeting under an open sky. We sat on the terrace of a small white church in Defence Colony. Ten peeling cane chairs set in a circle under the light of a single exposed bulb. The first person that caught my attention was this very petite girl in her late twenties. She wore running clothes, but she was covered in diamonds from head to toe. Next to her, a man with a briefcase full of stamp duty papers told me he had a job in the government. Next to him was a guy with a middle parting, wearing a black-and-white FILA sweatshirt. And next to him was a woman correcting school papers. As I glanced at her, I saw her scribble 'V. Good!' in red ink on the sheet she was holding.

It was a motley crew. None of these people looked like they would be friends or even speak to each other in another situation. I thought back to what Sukhi had said to me on our car ride. There is room in AA for people of all shades of belief and non-belief. This was not a members-only club. The only requirement was an honest desire to quit drinking. Sukhi was the sponsor for this group, something that happens only when you've applied the AA principles in your life long enough to support others.

Sukhi, the alcoholic, since he was effectively the master of this ceremony, opened the circle. 'My name is Sukhpal, and I'm an alcoholic.' We all know from countless films and TV shows that every AA meeting begins this way.

But as the introductions went around, I got increasingly nervous. Because every introduction was followed by a damning confession. But, and this is the most important part of my story, I was not an alcoholic.

There are two kinds of people in the world. Those that say, Why? and those that say, Why not? When Sukhi suggested I come to the meeting, it excited me, so I said, 'Why not?' But when he asked me to introduce myself as an alcoholic, I was scared. I asked, 'Why?'

'Because then you'll experience this evening in a way that you would never be able to otherwise. You like feeling things, right?'

I remember how deathly quiet it was. Perhaps because it was a weeknight. Perhaps it was because my heart was beating so loudly that I could barely hear anything else. But by the time the introductions went around the circle and it was my turn, I had decided that fear never made for a good story. So, I took a deep breath and began, 'My name is Eisha, and I'm an alcoholic.'

They all looked at me with complete trust and said, 'Hi Eisha. Welcome to AA.'

Whenever a new member joins, the others must tell the person their story. It's protocol. This helps the new person accept their situation, and acceptance is the first step towards change.

Briefcase started drinking as an adult just to keep up with the rest of his colleagues, except that he lost his job soon after, followed – in quick succession – by his wife and the rest of his family. He went to rehab, got sober, got a new job, a new wife and a new life, but when a bartender at a Diwali party accidentally added rum to his coke, he was right back to where he had started.

Diamonds was waking up every day at 4 a.m. to go to the thheka before her husband woke up. After he found bottles hidden in the oven, he took away her car keys. Then, desperate for her daily dose of poison, she managed to give herself a black eye to convince her parents that her husband had beaten her up so that she could move back to her parents' home and raid their bar. That's when I realized the only diamond missing from her was a wedding ring. The lady with the red pen had her wake-up call when she drove her car into a lamp post, while drunk. She realized how fortunate she had been to be alive.

Middle Parting had recently lost his father. He had died from the grief of having an addict for a son. The son realized he needed to fight his addiction just so he wouldn't lose his mom, too. But I never heard the end of his story because he was crying so hard that he couldn't finish what he was saying.

And I? I was just sitting there in that circle, listening to their stories, absolutely stunned. I kept wondering how these people could keep going back to the bottle despite the havoc it caused in their lives. Or was the opposite true? Was it easier to go back to it to drown the deepening sorrows? That's when Sukhi spoke. 'The most common misconception about an addiction is that it's a choice. Being drunk is a delightful state for an addict. Once real life becomes unbearable, once you get used to being drunk, it's difficult to stay sober. Alcohol helps you lose all fear. Can you imagine that feeling of no fear?' I couldn't. And then I realized he was looking straight at me when he said that. In fact, they were all looking at me. Because it was my turn to speak.

Earlier, whenever I sat in a circle listening to people's stories, I couldn't wait to tell my own. But tonight, I wondered if I had anything to say. These people trusted me, reopened their deepest wounds to acquaint me with their pain and help me heal in the process. They had relived their most painful memories because they knew something I didn't – that we always repeat what we don't repair. They knew so much better than me that grief doesn't need a reason, anxiety doesn't listen to logic, and trauma doesn't care how much time has elapsed. Alcohol may have made them fearless, but healing made them brave. And every single day they were trying to do a little bit better than they had yesterday. But that was more than I could say for myself.

I didn't say a word. I couldn't. I was absolutely paralysed. Because at that moment, I was acutely aware that it wasn't them who deserved to feel ashamed. It was me. Because every time before tonight, when I heard the word addict I tuned out the rest of the story. Before tonight, I didn't know that tolerance was just a very cheap form of respect. When I looked at them looking back at me, I saw that same flash of pride I had seen in Sukhi's eyes when he said, 'I'll always be an alcoholic, my dear. I just don't drink any more.' For me that's where his story ended, but for him, it was only the beginning.

Sharing in a meeting is a choice, and they thought I had made mine, so the meeting was called to a close without me saying anything. By the time we went downstairs, the alcoholics had swarmed around me – Briefcase, Diamonds, Red Pen and Middle Parting – all scribbling their numbers on any piece of paper they could find.

'You're one of us now.'

They told me that if I felt the urge to drink, I should call one of them that very second. Not so they could join me but so they could stop me.

'Call any time, Babe,' Diamonds said, 'I don't care if it's 4 a.m. You make sure you call me.'

I was still silent. On every level, I felt like an absolute fraud. Here I was, surrounded by more love than I had received in years, that too from strangers, and it all came out of a lie? What would happen when they found out the truth?

That's when Sukhi pulled me out of the group and shouted in a crude voice, 'Calm down, everyone. She's not an Alky! She just wanted to know what it was all about.'

The world around me froze. I stared back at them having no idea what to expect. Afraid of how they would react to my betrayal. Why would he do this to me? I waited for their response filled with dread.

But all they did was shrug and say, 'Okay.' And they headed back to their cars.

That's when I understood that this whole evening had nothing to do with me.

They didn't do this for me. They did this for themselves. They came back here every week because they knew better than me that you cannot heal in the same place you got sick.

We got back in the car, and I looked at him. Sukhi, the alcoholic who had a crude voice and talked too much. He was quiet for the first time tonight, staring out of the window. Then he spoke. Without even looking at me he said, 'Krishnamurti , I hope I see you as an actor one day.'

The people, characters and incidents that have been portrayed in this story are based on true events, but their identities have been altered to protect them because that's, in fact, what we all need to do, protect each other.

My name is Eisha. And I'm not an alcoholic.

Kopal's Takeaway

Eisha's story drew me in because it exudes empathy. It's a tough confession, yet it offers so much to the listener by showing how easily we judge others without truly knowing their story. While we can't live everyone's experiences or step into their shoes, this story gently reminds us to be kinder and more understanding. Everyone's journey is unique, and a little empathy can go a long way.

Story 22

I Was a Police Officer, But This Is My True Legacy

THAN SINGH

Growing up, all I knew was that a man in a police uniform had the power to create change. It had always been my father's lifelong dream to wear that uniform, but the weight of extreme poverty and family responsibilities kept him from achieving it. When I was born, his hope was rekindled; he began to believe that, one day, I might accomplish what he could not.

He worked day and night to make ends meet; I remember that he would wake up at 5 a.m. to go to work and make sure that my two sisters and I got a decent education.

When I was in Grade 6, I started working with my parents to support them. I used to iron clothes, wash them and even deliver them to the homes to which they belonged. Since I had afternoon school, I worked both before and after classes.

My father named me Than Singh, but everyone fondly called me Thanna. Despite all the time spent washing and ironing clothes, I always made sure to study whenever I could. Life wasn't easy – we struggled a lot because we didn't have much money. I still remember, as kids, all our friends used to talk about watching dramas on TV. We didn't have a TV, so my sisters and I would go to other people's jhuggis to watch it. The moment they realized we were watching it too, they would draw the curtain and we'd have to leave. On our way back to our jhuggi, I would hold my sisters' hands and tell them to have faith in me.

As I grew older, I realized I had to do more for the family; so I started selling corn (bhutta). By this time I had applied to the Delhi police twice and failed both times. People would taunt my father a lot during those years but he only encouraged me. He would tell me to never lose hope and keep going, and it was in my third attempt, in 2010, that I finally got selected. That day, I made a promise to myself – to do something meaningful for society and to wear my uniform with pride, leaving a mark that people would remember. That has been my goal since the day I joined.

This is where my journey from Thanna to becoming 'Police Wale Uncle' begins.

My duty was near the Lal Qila; and during my rounds, I would always notice young kids either selling plastic, begging or some even resorting to substance abuse. I couldn't just stand by and watch this happen in front of my eyes. So, one day, I decided to hear their story. They told me, 'Uncle ji, hum padhna chahte hain, lekin nahin padh paa rahe.' (Uncle ji, we want to study but we are not able to.)

These words stayed with me. I remembered my days, not too long ago, when I was selling bhuttas and ironing clothes as a 10-year-old. I felt like life had changed for me; why couldn't I play a part in changing the life of others?

I made a resolve to help them. I asked everyone where they stayed and started visiting their families. One by one I started convincing their parents to send the kids to school; some said it's pointless, some said they had no money, some said the kids needed to start earning money at a young age – it wasn't easy at all but I managed to convince the parents of five kids.

In 2015, I started Than Singh ki Paathshala. I started the school in the parking lot of the Lal Qila with five students. I couldn't bear the thought of seeing children have gutka (smokeless tobacco) and work in the heat to make ₹50. So my first goal was to help these children stop begging and selling garbage. I wanted to change their mindset; I wanted them to know that they could dream big and do more for their families if they spent their days learning.

I bought them notebooks, and every day we would sit in the parking lot and study together.

Slowly but steadily, I watched them change, and it gave me hope. That small paathshala became my way of giving back to society and fulfilling my promise to my uniform.

In 2020, when the COVID-19 pandemic hit, my only focus was to ensure they didn't fall back into begging, drugs or any distractions that could undo their progress.

As a police officer, I often had to visit hospitals for regular check-ups. At the time, officers diagnosed with COVID-19 were given ₹10,000 as aid. I used to think, if I test positive, I could use that money to help these kids. Every decision I made was driven by one goal – to create a better future for them.

By 2022, people started noticing my efforts. My seniors and team appreciated what I was doing and encouraged me to continue. Their support gave me a newfound confidence, a sense of purpose and validation that I was on the right path. I believed in these kids with all my heart and seeing them put all their faith in me made me feel like I had to reach more children.

As a police officer, I reached out to my seniors for help, and together we enrolled thirty more kids in my school.

Balancing my duty as a police officer and my commitment to these kids was never easy, but I found a way. Being a police officer helped – both the kids and their parents respected me, and perhaps even feared me a little. This fear worked in their favour because whenever a child missed school for two consecutive days, I would visit their homes and remind the parents of how important education was, insisting they send their kids back to school.

This journey was never one-sided – it was a bond of trust. These kids supported me just as much as I supported them. In 2022, when the results were out, 9 out of the 30 children topped their class.

Some of these kids came from heartbreaking circumstances – many had lost either their mother or father. I still remember how we used to hold events near a temple in the Lal Qila. The kids would come to pray, asking God to help their parents find jobs so they could continue studying. Miraculously, their prayers were often answered. One of the parents even got a job as a sweeper in that very temple, and their child went on to top the fourth and fifth grades. I will never be able to forget that moment in this lifetime.

One memory that still brings tears to my eyes is of a little girl named Neelu. Her father had passed away, and on Father's Day, while other children were making gifts and cards for their dads, she came to me, silent and hesitant. Later that night, around ten-thirty she called me. I asked her, 'Beta, kya hua? Bolo.' (Child, what happened? Tell me.) After a long pause, she softly said, 'Uncle ji, Happy Father's Day.' I was overwhelmed, I couldn't hold back my tears.

Today, my paathshala has grown to 105 children. I am their Police Wale Uncle, but also their father. These kids wait for me to cut their birthday cakes. No matter how late I arrive, they won't cut the cake until I'm there. Their love for me is humbling, to say the least. They believe 'Uncle ji humare liye bahut kuch karenge' (Uncle ji will do a lot for us.) And I've made it my life's mission to honour that trust. I've always been honest with them, sharing my own struggles, and I tell them one thing again and again: 'Bachhon, tum himmat mat harna.' (Kids, don't lose faith.)

There have been times when people close to me mocked my efforts. They'd say, 'Yeh kya drama kar rakha hai?' (What is this drama that you are doing?) Even on tough days, my own kids at home would get upset and tell me to go spend time with 'those kids'. But how could I ever abandon these children? They have so much faith in me, so much trust. I'm the one who showed them the dream of a better life – how could I ever break it? No matter what it takes, I will ensure their dreams come true.

There's a saying: 'Padhe likhe ko toh kalam koi bhi pakda dega, lekin jo kabhi padha na ho, usko kalam pakadwana sabse badi baat hai.' (Anyone can make an educated person hold a pen but to make someone who hasn't been educated, hold a pen – that's a big deal.) Education is like the milk of a lioness – those who drink it will roar louder and stronger. That's what I want for these children. They've given me the strength, the drive and the motivation to keep pushing forward.

Today, girls from Mata Sundari College come to teach these kids, and I now have over hundred volunteers helping me. Places like the Lal Qila and Rajghat have become hubs for their learning. Even their meals are taken care of, thanks to the Sis Ganj Gurdwara, which happily stepped in to provide food. Many of these children come from far-off places, and even the rickshaw drivers pitched in, offering to pick and drop them for free. The power of so many people coming together to help will create ripples I haven't even dreamt of. I know it.

To these kids, I always say one thing: 'Beta, himmat mat harna. Jab tak meri saans chalegi, main tumhare liye jeeyunga. Baaki uparwala dekhega.' (Child, don't lose courage. Till I am breathing, I will live for you. Rest I shall leave up to God.)

Kopal's Takeaway

I first met Than Singh ji when he narrated his story at one of our events in Delhi. He had come along with a few children from the paathshala, and it was such a joy to see an auditorium with 600 people stand up in unison after hearing his story. But the loudest cheers came from the children he had brought with him, their love and admiration for him unmistakable. Than Singh ji's story is truly special because it has taught me how the power of a single man's actions can create ripples far and wide, touching lives in ways we often cannot foresee.

Your Takeaways

Dear Reader, you can write down some of the special, personal things you may have learnt and observed here.

Acknowledgements

This section of the book holds a special place in my heart because, truthfully, I have very little to do with the creation of this book. These stories and the incredible people behind them have found their way into my life so magically over the past seven years that I feel like nothing more than a medium – helping their light reach more people.

From the very first story performed on Tape A Tale to the latest, I am endlessly in awe of the courage it takes for people to be vulnerable and share their raw, authentic selves. My deepest gratitude goes to everyone who trusted this book with their stories. It belongs to them.

I also want to thank every storyteller who has trusted me and Tape A Tale over the

ACKNOWLEDGEMENTS

years; choosing to open their hearts and share their truth. I've done my best to preserve their narratives, their language, their emotions, as they were shared with me – whether through Zoom calls or in-person meetings.

The journey of building Tape A Tale has never been a solo one, and I owe my gratitude to everyone who has been part of the team and contributed in any capacity along the way. A special shoutout to Ali Husen and Utkarsh Mehrotra – my partners in crime and rhyme during the early days of this adventure.

The curation, writing and editing of this book would not have been possible without the invaluable support of Pragya Jha, Deon Demamount, Shweta Sharma and Muskan Malhotra. Their dedication and creativity throughout the process made this journey both seamless and rewarding.

The idea for this book might have stayed in my head forever if not for Smita Khanna who pushed me to start writing it. A big shoutout to her for helping this book find its home.

ACKNOWLEDGEMENTS

A big shout-out to the incredibly talented Anushka Tripathi for her brilliant work in designing the cover of this book!

A heartfelt thanks to the team at Juggernaut for their kindness, gracious feedback and unwavering support. I hope this is just the beginning of many books to come.

Last, but by no means least, my family – without their constant cheering, none of this would mean anything. To my two sets of parents who somehow never tire of my updates about how the event went, how the book is shaping up or when my next shoot is (which, frankly, surprises me!). And to my husband, Ankit, who encourages me to dream bigger and is surprisingly okay with me sneaking in work during our holidays sometimes. And, of course, Kareshma, Pranav, Apeksha, Aditya and my adorable Anvay and Aarna – life feels so much simpler and brighter with family like you rooting for me.

To you, holding this book in your hands – thank you for picking it up and allowing these

ACKNOWLEDGEMENTS

stories the chance to touch your life. I hope these pages brought you hope, gratitude, and a little magic along the way. I hope you carry these stories with you like a lantern while walking through long dark nights. I hope you keep hoping. I hope.

A Note on the Author

Kopal Khanna is a storyteller, writer, producer and founder of Tape A Tale, one of the biggest storytelling platforms in the world today, with three million followers across social media. She also runs her own podcast, Qisse with Kopal. Kopal was awarded Creative Entrepreneur of the Year by Womennovator and was recognized in a list of top 20 women 'bizruptors' by Reliance Foundation's Her Circle. She is a history graduate from St. Stephen's College, Delhi, and has a master's degree in communication from the London School Of Economics and University of Southern California.